BREAKING the SUGAR HABIT Cookbook

Katherine M. Birkner, C.R.N.A., Ph.D.

Forward by Billie J. Sahley, Ph.D.

Pain & Stress Center Publications
San Antonio, Texas
1995

Note to Readers

This material is not intended to replace services of a physician, nor it is it meant to encourage diagnosis and treatment of illness, disease, or other medical problems by the layman. This book should not be regarded as a substitute for professional medical treatment and while every care is taken to ensure the accuracy of the content, the authors and the publisher cannot accept legal responsibility for any problem arising out of experimentation with the methods described. Any application of the recommendation set forth in the following pages is at the reader's discretion and sole risk. If you are under a physician's care for any condition, he or she can advise you as to whether this is appropriate for you.

This publication has been complied through research resources at the **Pain & Stress Center,** San Antonio, Texas 78229.

Second Edition

Printed in the U.S.A.
A Pain & Stress Center Publication

Additional copies may be ordered from:
Pain & Stress Center
5282 Medical Drive Suite 160
San Antonio, TX 78229-6043
(210) 614-7246

Library of Congress Catalog Card No. 90-81658
ISBN 0-9625914-1-6

FORWARD

Breaking The Sugar Addiction Habit Cookbook belongs in every home. This excellent publication was researched and written by my associate and practitioner of orthomolecular therapy at the Pain & Stress Center in San Antonio, Texas.

Dr. Birkner prepared this text to give a guideline for you and your family to stop your uncontrollable consumption of refined sugar. She has written the book so that the reader is able to follow a clear, concise cooking program to stop them as well as their families addiction to refined sugar.

In recent years there has been a steady accumulation of well documented studies indicating unequivocally that a diet high in sugar can cause behavior problems in adults and children. Hyperactivity, anxiety as well as depression are affected by sugar abuse and can predispose you to addiction. Universal awareness of this problem should be an ultimate goal among educators and health care professionals. Unfortunately, for many the purpose of eating has become centered on satisfying the taste of the tongue, and this is where the problem of sugar abuse begins.

Today, Americans are overfed and undernourished. Research has shown people eat their weight in sugar in one year. Given that fact, consider your child's intake. You are not only what you eat, but what is absorbed by your brain. This effects your mind, mood, memory and behavior.

Are you or your children addicted to sugar? After you read this book, you will be able to answer not only that question, but many others regarding sugar and your health.

Billie J. Sahley, Ph.D.
Executive Director
Pain & Stress Center

ACKNOWLEDGMENTS

My sincere appreciation and thanks to:

My associate, Dr. Billie J. Sahley for all her work, contributions, encouragement, and support.

My mother, Theresa Birkner, for insisting I learn to cook when I was young.

A special doctor, teacher, and healer, Doris Rapp, M.D., for sharing a world of information and knowledge.

The staff of the Pain & Stress Center of San Antonio, Texas (past and present) for their support and dedication to helping people.

Our patients, who teach us everyday.

CONTENTS

INTRODUCTION TO ADDICTION

How long has it been since you or your children had a sugar fix? Have you ever stopped to consider that you and your children might have a sugar addiction? The first step in breaking your sugar addiction is accepting the fact that you have one. Latest research suggests four out of every ten people are born with a potential for addiction. Sugar is at the top of the list as sugar is an *addictive* drug.

Denial of a possible addiction can render you unaware of how addiction can effect your life in a negative way. We all grow up with sugar; it surrounds us at birthdays, holidays and all happy occasions. You never think that you might be addicted or even allergic to sugar, or that sugar could cause hyperactive behavior, depression, A.D.D. (Attention Deficit Disorder).

Addiction can occur to any substance. You can be addicted to many foods. Ironically, the foods you like and crave the most are the foods that you could be allergic to or have a sensitivity to. People who do not have an addiction to sugar or display addictive behavior and feel in need of energy boost will often eat one of the many foods containing sugar, white flour or other refined carbohydrates. Often, after eating a reasonable amount of sugar-filled foods, they will feel satisfied for several hours. You might not feel any need to go back for more. A normal physiological hunger has been met and satisfied in a normal way.

But if you or your children have a sugar addiction, after eating a normal amount, you will want more. Your physiological hunger is not satisfied and continues to push you to eat more. Sometimes you binge, then feel depressed and guilty. Addiction to sugar is very powerful. In many people, sugar addiction is stronger and harder to overcome than alcohol.

Research has shown, we live a world of over consumption and under-nutrition. People seem to have an inborn attraction to sugar and sweet-tasting foods. Americans have become accustomed to the sweet taste of sugar from early childhood. Most people consume their weight in sugar each year. Foods are laden with sugar, and added to almost *every* processed food in some form. Sugar adds bulk, texture and body, and is so cheap it is used extensively in processing.

Processors can use unripe fruit in their canned products and chemically grown sweet corn which by itself does not much flavor and is not especially sweet to taste. Sugar is added and disguised by many names including sucrose, corn syrup, beet sugar, cane sugar, table sugar, corn syrup, malted barley, maltodextrin, malt syrup, brown sugar, glucose and dextrose. Instead of reducing sugar content in many foods, the processors substituted three or four types of sugar so that the word "sugar" would not appear as the number one ingredient on the label. It is hard to make *healthy* choices when so many choices are available.

Some people dislike honey, but honey is twice as sweet as cane sugar, and contains trace minerals void in sugar. Sugar is frequently produced from cane, a grass relative of wheat, corn or beets or a combination of the three.

This cookbook is your source book to freedom from sugar and healthier eating. I have included as much information as possible to help you and your children, especially if your child is hyperactive. Once you change your diet, the changes in behavior will be noticeable within days. You are what you eat and absorb. And when the brain is flooded with sugar, behavior reflects it.

What About Sugar and Hyperactive Child?

There are millions of children in the United States who suffer from some type of learning disability, hyperactivity, A.D.D. or hyperkinesis. Hyperactivity is often caused by physiological disorders such as chemical and nutritional imbalances, blood glucose disturbances, allergic reactions to foods and chemicals or poor diet. For more information read Dr. Sahley's book entitled, *The Natural Way To Control Hyperactivity.*

A child's state of health is his state of nutrition. Anyone can develop medical symptoms due to allergic reactions. Doris Rapp, M.D., pediatric allergist in Buffalo, New York treats many children with multiple symptoms of hyperactivity. In her book, *Is This Your Child?,* she describes medical symptoms due to allergic reactions. Dr. Rapp refers to these symptoms as the "allergic-tension fatigue syndrome." The physical symptoms include:

Nose: sneezing, year-round stuffiness, watery nose, nose rubbing (nose salute).

Aches: muscles, head, back, neck, growing pains or

	aches unrelated to exercise.
Belly problems:	nausea, upset stomach, bloating, bellyaches, bad breath, gaseous stomach, belching, vomiting, diarrhea, constipation
Bladder problems:	bedwetting or daytime wetting, need to rush to urinate, burning or pain with urination.
Face:	puffiness, below eyes , pale, dark eye circles.
Glands:	swelling of lymph nodes of neck.
Ear problems:	repeated formation of fluid behind eardrums, frequent ear infections, ringing ears, dizzi ness, excessive perspiration, low grade fever.

The following article, entitled "Kids and Sugar", appeared in the October, 1995 issue of the *Townsend Letter for Doctors & Patients:*

"Pediatric researchers at Yale University School of Medicine found that sugar causes a noticeable physiological reaction in normal healthy children. In the study, 25 children and 23 young adults were given the sugar equivalent to of two 12 ounce can of cola on a empty stomach while resting in bed. The researchers found that "blood sugar levels fell significantly further in the children than in the adults. More important, the children's adrenaline levels rose twice as high as the adults' and remained elevated during the five hours of scientific observation." The body releases adrenaline to counteract the effects of too much insulin and the resulting low blood sugar. The children's brain waves also showed that the ability to pay attention was affected. Although the physiological effects were clear, the researchers could not determine sugar's effects on behavior. They are planning another study to analyze behavioral effects."

Be more aware of your children's behavior after eating certain foods. During the same time, keep a log of your child's activities and what he eats. Be especially cognizant of the foods he eats or drinks and the amount of sugar or caffeine he consumes.

Dr. Janice Phelps in her book, *The Hidden Addiction And How To Get Free*, states that sugar addiction causes many symptoms that are not readily identified. Eventually addicted people express they do not feel as good as they should. Children can experience extreme reactions to sugar such as perpetual motion, aggressive behavior and constant talking. Marked improvement can be seen when the sugar is withdrawn, and the diet is supported with complex carbohydrates and the proper amino acids, vitamins, minerals and protein. A good amino acid, vitamin and mineral program is very important when withdrawing sugar.

Sugar addiction is probably the world's most widespread addiction and the hardest to break. "Sugar addiction" refers to simple or refined carbohydrates. Simple sugars are absorbed and enter the bloodstream very rapidly. Complex carbohydrates enter the body more slowly, and do not invoke hyperactive symptoms as simple sugar does. But sugar upsets your *whole* body chemistry

Dr. Phelps believes sugar addictions the "basic addiction" as it is so widespread. It is shared by so many children and adults. Sugar addiction precedes all other addictions. Sugar dysmetabolism is the primary factor in profile for addiction. Sugar can last a lifetime, or the person can progress to other addictive substances such as prescription or street drugs.

Most addictive people experience other symptoms as a direct result of their manufacturing sugar metabolism. Children who are addicted to sugar experience mood swings plus anxiety and depression. As they are get older they are more likely to try hard drugs. The sugar predisposes them to addictive behavior.

The amino acid, glycine, has been used successfully to help break a sugar addiction. Glycine is the simplest nonessential amino acid, and considered to be the third major neurotransmitter in the brain. An inhibitory neurotransmitter is a substance in the brain that slows down the speed of transmission of anxiety related messages between brain cells. Glycine has a calming effect. It is a beneficial "sweetener." It has a sweet taste and is very soluble in water. Glycine is an excellent substance for sugar for hyperactive children and for people that want to restrict their sugar intake. Glycine is non-toxic. The only reported side effect is possible loose stool. Glycine is available in capsules or powder. It can be sprinkled over a piece of fruit or on a muffin or mixed with cereal to help cut the sugar craving. It adds sweetness at the same time. Unfortunately, it cannot be substituted in baked goods. For more information on amino acids and hyperactivity, read Dr. Billie Sahley's book, *The Natural Way To Control Hyperactivity.*

Another way to reduce the craving for sugar according to the book, *Sugar Chemistry,* is by the administration of Gymnema sylvestre. Gymnema sylvestre is a herb that obliterates sweetness so that sugar tastes like sand. Gymnema sylvestre is available in capsule form. It is safe for children.

What Is Hypoglycemia?

Classic hypoglycemia or low blood sugar does not commonly occur. But reactive or functional hypoglycemia occurs more frequently. Whenever you eat sugar in any form especially carbohydrates, starches or sugar, you feel like you get a lift. Your energy increases as your blood sugar rises. The increased blood sugar goes to all parts of your body including your heart, muscles and brain. But this rise is only temporary as your pancreas releases insulin in response to increased blood sugar or glucose. Insulin helps metabolize or burn the glucose and bring the glucose to a "normal" level.

Ingestion of sweets and other refined carbohydrates stimulates the pancreas to release insulin. If too much insulin is released, hypoglycemia can result. A drop in blood glucose to abnormally low levels causes symptoms of hypoglycemia. These include mood swings, fatigue, depression, headaches, nervousness, irritability, sweating, weakness, sleep disturbances and shakiness. With the ingestion of highly sugared foods or drink a yo-yo pattern can result.

Hypoglycemia can be very tricky and when food allergies are part of the problem multiple symptoms can occur. If the standard glucose tolerance is performed, it can be perfectly normal. But if a person is allergic to a specific food such as corn, and dextrose is used (dextrose is made from corn, and is commonly used in glucose tolerance tests) an abnormal glucose tolerance test can result. Allergic reactions to specific foods can cause abnormal blood sugar levels, and the behavior of a child or adult can be irrational.

Hypoglycemia is thought to occur prior to the onset of diabetes. If you want to regulate your blood sugar, you

---

Hypoglycemia Yo-yo Pattern

Ingestion of Sugared Food -> Outpouring of Insulin->
Low Blood Sugar -> Urge To Eat To Increase Blood Sugar
(Usually Highly Sugared) -> More Insulin Release ->
Decreased Blood Sugar -> Cycle Repeats

should eat a lot of whole grains, complex carbohydrates, vegetables and fiber. Avoid or rotate foods you know are the offenders. Seek help from a physician, an allergist or an orthomolecular therapist utilizing food allergy testing to help reduce reactions to foods. The test can be conclusive as to the level of sensitivity of each food.

Sugar seems to contribute to many behavior problems, hyperactivity, A.D.D, mood swings, depression and can contribute to obesity, elevated triglycerides and cholesterol, and heart disease. Excess refined sugar intakes pressures the body into converting the sugar into fatty acids called triglycerides. This kind of fatty acids are the saturated, sticky type that increases the risk of stroke, heart attack and arteriosclerosis. In addition, the excess sugar causes the body to produce more cholesterol.

Many factors should be explored as *many* factors are usually involved in all problems. Look at the *power* of sugar addiction. Sugar is in many of the foods that you eat everyday. Read labels--sugar is disguised by many names.

Most people say, "I can give up sugar anytime I want to." But for how long? *Keep a sugar diary including everything they eat and drink for a week. Check off all the items containing sugar, either added by the food processing or by yourself. Then try not to eat any refined sugar or simple sugar in any form, food or drink for 21 days.* See how you feel? Remember, you have to want to get off sugar. You can experience some withdrawal effects. Sugar withdrawal symptoms include anxiety, depression, hyperactivity, inability to concentrate, irritability, anger tremors, weakness, muscle contraction headaches, blurred vision and rapid heartbeat.

Serving sugary sweets to children can setup an eating pattern will follow them for a lifetime. Many children that are given sweets often develop excess fat cells and malfunctioning glands. This leads to problems with weight control and their continued craving for sweets. Many become psychologically dependent on sugar. If they become depressed or lonely, they reach for sweets. This can lead to a life-long behavior pattern. Malfunctioning glands do not secrete sufficient hormones can result in obesity, hypoglycemia, diabetes, improper growth, heart disease, depression, hyperactivity, etc.

A new theory from Richard Bergland, M.D., in his book, *Fabric of the Mind,* postulates the brain is a hormonally modulated gland. Emotions spill hormones and catecholamines (like adrenaline or norepinephrine) into the brain affecting our behavior. Sugar highs and lows have a direct effect on brain chemistry and behavior.

The immune system is depleted by sugar. Sugar breeds bacteria in the mouth promoting tooth decay and periodontal disease. In the intestine, sugar promotes the growth of yeast, contributing to yeast infections. Sugar robs the body of the B vitamins.

But glucose (blood sugar) is found in the blood of every animal and is necessary for life. Glucose is used as energy by the muscles, brain and organs in the body. But you do not have to eat sugar to obtain it. Complex carbohydrates such as starches are made up of glucose that must be broken down by the digestive system. Complex carbohydrates are usually high in fiber, and fiber slows down the rate of sugar absorption into the body. Complex carbohydrates are digested over several hours. This allows for a slow release/absorption of the glucose so the blood sugar is maintained at a normal level without peaks and valleys yielding the yo-yo cycle.

Sugar is virtually void of all nutrients. Every one-fourth cup of sugar, whether white, brown or turbinate, adds about 200 empty calories to your recipes. Decrease the sugar in recipes by adding more cinnamon, nutmeg, vanilla, almond, etc. to enhance the flavors. Certain fruits such as apples, bananas, pears, dates and figs naturally sweeten recipes by themselves. Try adding some to your favorite recipe and decreasing the sugar.

You may wonder whether decreasing sugar will sacrifice palatability. Whittling away the sugar, fat and salt will not necessarily detract from the taste. Foods may taste delightfully different and will not be as rich. Your palate will become accustomed to the taste rapidly, and will come to prefer the new, lighter taste.

The recipes in this book offer a healthy alternative to traditional highly sugared foods. Use it as a basis for good nutrition and a happier, healthier lifestyle to free you from the addictiveness of sugar.

If you need help with your sugar addiction, see a behavior therapist who is trained to help those who need help altering negative behavior patterns.

SUGAR CONTENT IN COMMON FOODS

Food	Serving Size	Sugar / Tsp.
Beverages		
Cola	12 oz.	7
Ginger ale	12 oz.	10
Root Beer	10 oz.	10
Orange	12 oz.	7.5
Seven-Up	12 oz.	7.5
Cider	1 cup	6
Whiskey	3 oz.	1.5
Cakes		
Angel Food	4 oz.	7
Applesauce	4 oz.	5.5
Banana	2 oz.	2
Chocolate (plain)	4 oz.	6
Chocolate (iced)	4 oz.	10
Cheese	4 oz.	2
Coffee	4 oz.	4.5
Cupcake with icing	1	6
Fruit	4 oz.	5
Orange	4 oz.	4
Pound	4 oz.	5
Sponge	1 oz.	2
Strawberry Shortcake	1	4
Cookies		
Brownies	3/4 oz.	3
Chocolate	1	1.5
Fig Newton	1	5
Gingersnaps	1	3
Macaroons	1	6
Nut	1	1.5
Oatmeal	1	2
Sugar	1	1.5
Donuts		
Chocolate Eclair	1	7
Cream Puff	1	2
Donut (Plain)	1	3
Donut (Glazed)	1	6
Candies		
Hershey Bar	1.5 oz.	2.5
Chocolate Cream	1	2
Chocolate Mints	1	2
Fudge	1 oz.	4.5
Gumdrop	1	2
Hard Candy	4 oz.	20
Lifesavers	1	1/3

Food	Serving Size	Sugar / Tsp.
Peanut Brittle	1 oz.	3.5
Fruits / Juices Canned in Sugar		
Fruit Juice	1/2 cup	2
Peaches	1/2 cup	3.5
Fruit Salad	1/2 cup	3.5
Fruit Syrup	2 Tbsp.	2.5
Dairy Products		
Ice Cream	3.5 pz.	3.5
Ice Cream Bar	1	1.7
Ice Cream Cone	1	3.5
Ice Cream Soda	1	5
Ice Cream Sundae	1	7
Malted Milk Shake	10 oz.	5
Sherbet	4 oz.	9
Jellies and Jams		
Jelly	1 oz.	4.5
Orange Marmalade	1 oz.	4.5
Apple Butter	1 oz.	1
Strawberry Jam	1 oz.	4
Miscellaneous		
Chewing Gum	1 stick	1/2
Apple Cobbler	1/2 cup	3
Blueberry Cobbler	1/2 cup	3
Cherry pie	slice	10
Custard	1/2 cup	2
French Pastry	4 oz.	5
Jello	1/2 cup	4.5

BREADS

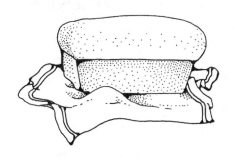

BREADS

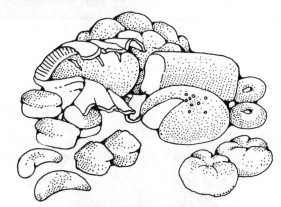

BREADS

APRICOT BREAD

1/3 cup boiling water
1 cup chopped apricots
2 cups whole wheat or spelt flour *or*
    7/8 cup rice + 1 cup amaranth *or* barley flour
2 tsp. baking powder
1/2 tsp. baking soda
1/2 tsp. salt
1/3 cup honey
1/4 cup canola or sunflower oil
1 egg or 2 egg whites
1/2 cup white grape juice concentrate

Preheat oven. Spray 9" X 5" x 3" loaf pan with vegetable spray. Pour boiling water over dates. Let cool to lukewarm. Mix dry ingredients together. Beat honey, oil and egg until creamy. Add grape juice to lukewarm date mixture. Alternating, add dry ingredients and grape juice mixture to creamy mixture. Mix well after each addition. Pour into loaf pan. Bake 45 minutes or until toothpick inserted into center of loaf comes out clean. Cool on rack. Remove from pan after 10 minutes.

Yield: 1 loaf
Oven: 350°F.
Time: 45 minutes

RICE BREAD

1 1/4 cups reconstituted non-fat dry milk, scalded
1/4 cup safflower oil
1 tsp. salt
2 Tbsp. honey
3 cups cooked long grain rice
2 packages active dry yeast
2 cups unbleached flour
2 cups whole wheat flour

Pour 1 cup milk over oil, honey and salt, stir. Add to cooked rice. Dissolve yeast in 1/4 cup milk that has cooled, then stir into rice mixture. Work in flour to make a firm dough. Turn out onto a floured board and knead until smooth and elastic. Place in greased bowl, turn to grease top, cover, and let rise until double in bulk. Punch down and knead for 2-3 minutes, then shape into 2 small loaves. Place in well-greased loaf pans, cover and let rise until double in bulk. Brush top with melted margarine, then bake at 375°F. for 40-45 minutes until golden brown.

Yield: 2 loaves
Oven: 375°F.
Time: 40-45 minutes

DATE BREAD

1/3 cup boiling water
1 cup chopped dates
1 cup rice flour
1 cup barley *or* whole wheat flour
2 tsp. baking powder
1/2 tsp. baking soda
1/2 tsp. salt
1/3 cup honey
1/4 cup canola or sunflower oil
1 egg or 2 egg whites
1/2 cup nonfat dry milk liquid

Preheat oven. Spray 9" X 5" x 3" loaf pan with vegetable spray. Pour boiling water over dates. Let cool to lukewarm. Mix dry ingredients together. Beat honey, oil and egg until creamy. Add milk to lukewarm date mixture. Alternately, add dry ingredients and milk mixture to creamy mixture. Mix well after each addition. Pour into loaf pan. Bake 45 minutes or until toothpick inserted into center of loaf comes out clean. Cool on rack. Remove from pan after 10 minutes.

Yield: 1 loaf
Oven: 350°F.
Time: 45 minutes

BANANA NUT BREAD

1 1/4 cups unbleached flour
1 1/4 cups whole wheat flour
1 tsp. salt
1/4 cup canola or safflower oil
1/4 tsp. non-fat dry milk, reconstituted
1 egg or egg substitute
1/3 cup honey
3-4 very ripe bananas
1 cup raisins
1 cup chopped pecans or walnuts
4 tsp. baking powder

In large bowl, mix flours, baking powder and salt. Blend oil, milk, egg, honey, and bananas in blender, then add to dry ingredients. Fold in raisins and nuts. Turn into a large 9"X 5" X 3" greased loaf pan. Bake until toothpick comes out clean.

Yield: 1 large loaf
Oven: 350°F.
Time: 55 minutes

OAT BANANA BREAD

1 cup oat flour
1 cup oat bran
1/4 cup rolled oats
1/2 tsp. salt
1/4 cup safflower oil
1 1/2 cups mashed ripe bananas (about 3)
1/4 cup honey
2 eggs
1 tsp. vanilla

Combine flour, bran oats, baking soda and salt. Make a well in center of mixture. Combine bananas, honey, oil, eggs, and vanilla. Add to dry ingredients, stirring just until moistened. Coat 9" X 5" X 3" loaf pan with cooking spray. Spoon batter into pan. Bake at 350°F. for 1 hour or until toothpick inserted in center comes out clean.

Yield: 1 loaf
Oven: 350°F.
Time: 1 hour

PEAR NUT BREAD

2 fresh, fully ripe pears
2 large eggs, beaten
1 cup whole bran
3/4 cup unbleached flour
3/4 cup whole wheat flour
1/4 cup honey
1 tsp. salt
1/2 tsp. baking soda
1/4 cup canola oil
1/2 cup chopped walnuts

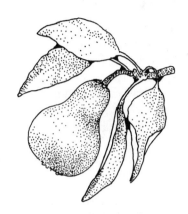

Core and finely chop <u>unpeeled</u> pears to measure 1 1/4 cups. Combine with eggs and bran; let stand while preparing rest of ingredients.

Sift flour with baking powder, salt and soda into mixing bowl. Add oil and pear-bran mixture mixing until all of flour is moistened. Stir in walnuts. Turn into a well-greased 9" X 5" X 3" loaf pan. Let stand 30 minutes, then bake about 1 hour or until toothpick into center comes out clean. Let stand 10 minutes, then turn out onto wire rack to cool. If desired, spread with Lemon Mint Butter.

Yield: 1 loaf
Oven: 350°F.
Time: 1 hour

Lemon Mint Butter
Beat 1 cup softened butter or margarine with 1 teaspoon grated lemon peel and 2 tablespoons chopped fresh mint leaves.

CARROT BREAD

3 cups carrot juice or vegetable water at 115°F.
1/4 cup honey
3 Tbsp. active dry yeast
2 tsp. salt
3 Tbsp. canola *or* safflower oil
1/2 cup wheat germ
1/2 cup gluten flour
8 cups whole wheat flour *or*
   4 cups unbleached and 4 cups whole wheat flour
2 cups carrots

Add honey to carrot juice, stir in yeast, and cover; let stand 10 minutes or until yeast is bubbly. Add salt and oil. Mix wheat germ and gluten flour with 5 cups whole wheat flour *or* 2 1/2 cups unbleached flour and 2 1/2 cups whole wheat flour. Then add flour mixture to yeast and beat well. Cover with a cloth and set to rise 10 minutes.

Stir in carrots and add flour, a cup at a time until dough is workable. Knead on a floured board 10 minutes. Place dough in oiled bowl, turning to oil dough, cover and set to rise in warm place for 45 minutes or until double in bulk.

Punch dough down, then turn onto a floured board and let rest for 10 minutes. During interval, grease 3 bread pans. Knead dough 3-4 turns. Form 3 loaves and place loaves seam side down in pans; cover and let rise another 45 minutes. After 35 minutes, heat oven to 375°F. Bake at 375°F. for 20 minutes, then lower heat to 300°F. and bake about 30 minutes longer or until double. Remove from pans and cool on wire rack.

Yield: 3 loaves
Oven: 375°F. / 300°F.
Time: 20 minutes / 30 minutes

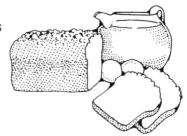

BROWN BREAD

1 1/4 cups whole wheat flour
1 1/4 cups unbleached flour
1/2 cup cornmeal
1 tsp. baking soda

8 oz. can crushed pineapple
1 cup very ripe bananas, mashed (about 3)
1 cup nonfat buttermilk
1/3 cup honey
3/4 cup dried apricots, chopped
1/2 cup pecans or walnuts, chopped

Coat four 1 pound cans with vegetable spray. Combine dry ingredients in large bowl. Add pineapple with juice, banana, buttermilk and honey, stirring just until dry ingredients are moistened. Fold in apricots and nuts. Pour evenly into 4 cans. Bake just until toothpick comes out clean. Remove from oven and allow to cool 10 minutes before inverting loaves onto a wire rack. Cool Slice. Serve.

Yield: 4 loaves
Oven: 300°F.
Time: 45 minutes

PUMPKIN GINGERBREAD

1 cup unbleached flour
1 cup whole wheat flour
1 cup whole grain cornmeal
1 tsp. baking soda
2 tsp. ginger
1 tsp. allspice
1 cup pumpkin, cooked and mashed *or* sweet potato
1 1/2 cups apple juice concentrate
1/2 cup honey
3/4 cup raisins

Coat 2 loaf pans with vegetable spray. Combine dry ingredients; mix well. Add pumpkin, apple juice concentrate and honey, stirring just until the dry ingredients are moistened. Fold in raisins. Pour into loaf pans and bake until toothpick inserted in center comes out clean. Remove from oven and allow to cool 10 minutes before turning loaves onto a wire rack.

Yield: 2 loaves
Oven: 350°F.
Time: 40-45 minutes

POTATO ROLLS

1 pkg. active dry yeast
1/4 cup warm water
1/4 cup warm milk
1/2 cup mashed potatoes
1 Tbsp. honey
1/2 tsp. salt
1/3 cup margarine, softened
1 1/4 cups whole wheat flour
1 1/4 cups unbleached flour

Dissolve yeast in warm water. (Note: If the water is too hot, it will kill the yeast. An easy way to obtain the correct temperature is to pour some over your forearm. If the water does not feel too hot or too cold, the water temperature is just right). Combine milk, potatoes, honey and salt. Add yeast and margarine. Mix in enough flour to make the dough easy to handle. Turn onto a floured board. Knead dough (adding more flour, if needed) until is feels smooth. Roll into a ball of dough 1 inch in diameter. Place 3 in a greased muffin tin. Brush with butter. Let rise until double in size (about 1 hour). Bake at 400°F. for 15 to 20 minutes or until golden brown.

Yield: 1 dozen
Oven: 400°F.
Time: 15-20 minutes

MUFFINS

MUFFINS

MUFFINS

APPLE OAT BRAN MUFFINS

1 1/2 cups oat bran
1/4 cup nonfat dry milk liquid
1/4 cup whole wheat flour
1 egg *or* egg substitute
1/4 cup unbleached flour
2 Tbsp. safflower oil
2 tsp. baking powder
2 Tbsp. honey
1/2 tsp. salt
1 cup cooking apples, peeled, cored and finely chopped
2 Tbsp. raisins
1/2 cup apple juice concentrate
1 Tbsp. cinnamon

Heat oven to 400 degrees F. Grease a 12 cup muffin pan or use paper liners. Combine oat bran, flours, baking powder, salt and cinnamon and set aside. In a large bowl, combine apple juice concentrate, skim milk, egg, sunflower oil and honey. Add flour mixture, apples and raisins, then combine until just moistened. Fill muffin tin and bake for about 20 minutes or until golden brown and a toothpick comes out clean.

Yield: 12 muffins
Oven: 400°F.
Time: 20 minutes

APPLE SPICE MUFFINS

1 cup unbleached flour
3/4 cup whole wheat flour
1/4 cup wheat germ
1 Tbsp. baking powder
1/2 tsp. salt
1/2 tsp. pumpkin pie spice
1/2 tsp. cinnamon
1/8 tsp. nutmeg
3/4 cup golden raisins

1 large egg
1/4 cup canola or safflower oil
2/3 cup frozen apple juice concentrate
1 tsp. vanilla extract
1 Tbsp. fresh grated lemon peel
1 cup apples, peeled, cored and minced

In large bowl combine flours, wheat germ, baking powder, salt, pumpkin pie spice, cinnamon, nutmeg and raisins. Peel and mince apple; set aside. In medium bowl beat egg lightly; stir in apples, oil, juice concentrate, vanilla and lemon peel. Add moist mixture to dry mixture all at once and stir until batter is moistened but lumpy. Spray muffin tin with vegetable spray. Fill cups with batter. Bake at 425°F. for 20-25 minutes.

Yield: 12
Oven: 425°F.
Time: 20-25 minutes

CRISPY RICE MUFFINS

1/2 cup "quick" brown rice
1 1/4 cups water
2 egg whites, beaten
1 Tbsp. sunflower oil
1/4 tsp. salt, if desired
2 tsp. honey
1 cup soymilk *or* nonfat dry milk liquid
2 tsp. baking powder
1 1/4 cups brown rice flour

Cook rice in water and salt over medium high heat for 10 minutes, then reduce to low for 2 more minutes. While rice is cooking, mix dry ingredients together, set aside. Stir rice into liquids, then add dry ingredients. Fill paper lined muffin tins and bake at 375°F. for 30-35 minutes.

Yield: 10
Oven: 375°F.
Time: 30-35 minutes

OAT BRAN MUFFINS

1 1/2 cups old fashioned oats
4 1/2 cups oat bran (1 lb.)
1 tsp. salt
2 Tbsp. baking powder
12 oz. can unsweetened apple juice concentrate, thawed
1/4 cup hot water
1/2 cup raisins
1 cup dried apples, chopped into small pieces
1/3 cup honey
4 eggs *or* 5 egg whites, lightly beaten
1/4 cup canola or sunflower oil
2 Tbsp. cinnamon

Mix all dry ingredients together in large mixing bowl. Mix raisins into apple juice concentrate, soaking 5-10 minutes to soften more. Measure oil, place in small bowl, then add eggs and honey, beating until mixed. Then add this to the dry ingredients, mixing only until moist. Fold in chopped apples. Place in greased muffin tins, filling 3/4 full. Bake until golden brown and toothpick comes out clean.

Yield: 2 1/2 dozen
Oven: 350⁰F.
Time: 15-20 minutes

APPLESAUCE MUFFINS

1 large egg
2 Tbsp. canola or safflower oil
1 1/2 cups unsweetened applesauce
1 cup unbleached flour
1 cup whole wheat flour
3/4 tsp. baking soda
2 tsp. baking powder
1/2 tsp. nutmeg
1 tsp. cinnamon
1 cup raisins

Beat together egg, oil and applesauce. Add flours, baking soda, baking powder, nutmeg and cinnamon, beating well. Stir in raisins. Spray muffin pan with vegetable spray, then flour. Bake for 20-25 minutes or until firm to the touch and browned. Cool on wire rack.

Yield: 12
Oven: 375°F.
Time: 20-25 minutes

BANANA NUT MUFFINS

2 1/4 cups oat bran
1 Tbsp. baking powder
1/4 cup honey
1/4 cup chopped pecans or walnuts
1 1/4 cups nonfat dry milk, reconstituted
2 very ripe bananas (the riper, the better)
2 egg whites
2 Tbsp. canola or vegetable oil

Preheat oven. Mix the dry ingredients in large bowl. Mix the milk, bananas, egg whites, and oil in bowl, then add to dry ingredients, mixing well. Line the muffin tin with paper baking cups or spray with vegetable oil, then fill with batter. Bake for 17 minutes.

Yield: 12 muffins
Oven: 425°F.
Time: 17 minutes

VARIATION:
Substitute 1 cup unsweetened apple juice or pineapple juice concentrate for milk, and decrease honey to 2 Tbsp.

CINNAMON APPLESAUCE MUFFINS

1 1/4 cups oat bran, uncooked
1 cup whole wheat flour
4 tsp. cinnamon
1 tsp. baking powder
3/4 tsp. soda
1/2 tsp. salt (optional)
3/4 cup unsweetened applesauce
1/3 cup honey
1/4 cup safflower or canola oil
1 egg
1 tsp. vanilla
1/4 cup chopped nuts or raisins

Heat oven. Spray muffin tins with a vegetable spray. In medium bowl, combine oat bran, flour, cinnamon, baking powder, baking soda and salt. In large bowl, combine applesauce, honey, oil, egg and vanilla. Stir in dry ingredients, mixing well. Add nuts or raisins. Fill muffin tins almost full. Bake. Serve warm.

Yield: 12
Oven: 375°F.
Time: 15-20 minutes

HONEY OATMEAL MUFFINS

2/3 cup non-fat dry milk liquid
1/3 cup vegetable oil
1 egg, beaten
1/3 cup honey
1 1/2 cups old fashioned rolled oats
1/2 cup unbleached flour
1/2 cup whole wheat flour
1/2 cup raisins
1/2 cup chopped walnuts or pecans (optional)
3/4 cup chopped dried apples
2 Tbsp. cinnamon

1 Tbsp. baking powder
1/2 tsp. salt

Combine milk, oil, egg, and honey. Combine remaining ingredients in large mixing well. Add liquid mixture to dry ingredients; mix just enough until dry ingredients are moistened. Grease muffin tins; fill cups 2/3 full. Bake at 400°F. 15-18 minutes or until golden brown and toothpick inserted comes out clean.

Yield: 1 dozen
Bake: 400°F.
Time: 15-18 minutes

PINEAPPLE MUFFINS

1/2 cup sunflower margarine
3 large eggs
20 oz. can crushed pineapple, drained, save juice
1 tsp. lemon juice
1 1/4 cups unbleached flour
1 1/4 cups whole wheat flour
1 tsp. baking soda
2 tsp. baking powder

In mixing bowl beat together butter, eggs, pineapple and lemon juices. Add flours, baking soda and baking powder, beating well. Stir in crushed pineapple. Spoon batter into greased and floured muffin tin. Bake at 350°F. for 20 minutes or until lightly browned. Cool on wire rack.

Yield: 1 dozen
Oven: 350°F.
Time: 20 minutes

OAT APPLE MUFFINS

1 1/2 cups oat bran
1/4 cup unbleached flour
1/4 cup whole wheat flour
5 Tbsp. honey
2 tsp. baking powder
1/2 tsp. salt
2 tsp. cinnamon
1/2 cup apple juice concentrate
1/4 cup milk *or* add 1/4 cup more apple juice concentrate
1 egg *or* egg substitute
2 Tbsp. canola or safflower oil
1 cup cooking apples, peeled, cored, and diced or grated
2-4 Tbsp. raisins

Preheat oven. Spray a 12 cup muffin tin with vegetable spray. Combine oat bran, flour, baking powder, salt, cinnamon, then set aside. In a large mixing bowl, combine egg, apple juice concentrate, milk or more concentrate, oil and honey. Add flour mixture, apples and raisins and combine until *just* moistened. Fill muffin tins. Bake for 20 minutes or until golden brown and toothpick comes out clean.

Yield: 12 muffins
Oven: 400⁰F.
Time: 18-20 minutes

NO FAT MUFFINS

3/4 cup whole wheat flour
3/4 cup unbleached flour
1 cup oat bran
2 1/2 tsp. baking powder
1/4 tsp. salt
1/4 tsp. allspice
1 tsp. cinnamon, if desired
2 egg whites, lightly beaten
2 Tbsp. honey
1 1/2 cups apple juice

Mix flours, oat bran, baking powder, salt and allspice together. Mix egg whites, honey and juice thoroughly, then stir into dry ingredients, but stirring only until mixed. Fill paper lined muffin tin about 2/3 full. Bake until cake toothpick inserted in the center comes out clean. Remove from tin and cool on wire rack.

Yield: dozen
Oven: 400°F.
Time: 30 minutes

RAISIN APPLESAUCE MUFFINS

1 large egg or egg substitute
2 Tbsp. canola or safflower oil
1 1/2 cups unsweetened applesauce
1 cup whole wheat flour
1 cup unbleached flour
3/4 tsp. baking soda
2 tsp. baking powder
2 tsp. cinnamon
1/2 tsp. nutmeg
3/4 cup golden raisins

Beat together egg, oil and applesauce. Add flours, baking soda, baking powder, cinnamon and nutmeg. Mix in raisins. Prepare muffin tin by spraying vegetable spray. Spoon batter into muffin tin. Bake until golden brown and firm. Cool on wire racks. Enjoy!!

Yield: 12
Oven: 375°F.
Time: 20-25 minutes

33

GINGERY OAT BRAN MUFFINS

2 cups oat bran
2 tsp. baking powder
1 tsp. ginger
1 tsp. cinnamon
1/4 tsp. cloves
3/4 cup unsweetened apple juice
1/4 cup applesauce
1/4 cup honey or molasses
2 Tbsp. canola or safflower oil
1 egg or 1/4 cup egg substitute
1/2 cup raisins

Mix dry ingredients together in large bowl. Separate eggs. Combine apple juice, applesauce, honey, oil, and egg yolk (if using eggs). Beat egg white or if using egg substitute, beat egg substitute to soft peaks and fold in. Carefully, fold in raisins. Line 8 large muffin cups with paper liners, then spoon in muffin mixture. (They will be full.) Bake for 20 minutes at 400°F. Remove from pan to cool *completely* before eating. This mellows the flavors and makes liners easier to remove. Muffins will stick when hot.

Yield: 8 large muffins
Oven: 400°F.
Time: 20 minutes

VARIATION: Substitute 1/2 cup finely chopped or grated apples for raisins or add 1/4 cup apples and 1/4 cup raisins or substitute 1/2 cup carob chips for raisins.

CRAN-APPLE MUFFINS

1 cup unbleached flour
1 cup whole wheat flour
1 Tbsp. baking powder
1/4 tsp. baking soda
3/4 tsp. cinnamon
1/2 cup apple juice concentrate, thawed
1/4 cup nonfat buttermilk

1/3 cup raisins
2 Tbsp. honey
1 egg, slightly beaten or 2 egg white, lightly beaten
1 cup apple, shredded (about 1 1/2 medium apples)
2 Tbsp. dried cranberries

Soak cranberries and raisins in apple juice concentrate for
5-10 minutes. Spray muffin pan with cooking spray. Combine dry ingredients in large bowl, mixing well. Add honey,
buttermilk, egg and apples to apple juice mixture, stirring.
Pour into dry ingredients, stirring just until moistened. Fill
muffin cups 3/4 full. Bake until toothpick inserted in center
comes out clean.

Yield: 12
Oven: 350⁰F.
Time: 15-20 minutes

ALMOND DATE MUFFINS

1 3/4 cup unbleached flour
1/2 cup date sugar
1 Tbsp. baking powder
1 cup nonfat buttermilk
1 egg, slightly beaten *or* 2 egg whites
1 tsp. almond extract
3/4 cup dates, finely chopped
1/4 cup + 1 Tbsp. almonds, finely chopped
1 tsp. date sugar

Topping: Combine teaspoon of date sugar and tablespoon of
almonds in small bowl. Set aside. Coat muffin tin with
cooking spray.

Combine dry ingredients in large bowl. Add moist ingredients to dry, stirring just until moistened. Fold in dates.
Sprinkle topping over batter. Bake until toothpick comes out
clean. Allowing muffins to cool for 5 minutes before removing from tins.

Yield: 12
Oven: 350⁰F.
Time: 18-20 minutes

ALMOND MUFFINS

2 cups rice flour
1 Tbsp. baking powder
1 Tbsp arrowroot
1/4 cup honey or maple syrup
1 tsp. almond extract
1 1/4 cups milk, soymilk or water
2 Tbsp. canola or safflower oil
1/2 cup almond, finely chopped + 1/4 cup for tops

Combine flour, baking powder, arrowroot and almonds in large bowl. In separate bowl combine honey, almond extract, milk, oil, then pour into dry ingredients, mixing thoroughly. Spray muffin tins with vegetable spray. Fill each tin about 3/4 full and sprinkle top with almond pieces. Bake.

Yield: 12 muffins
Oven: 350⁰F.
Time: 25-30 minutes

CORNMEAL MUFFINS

2 cups whole grain cornmeal
1/2 tsp. baking soda
2 tsp. baking powder
2 eggs, slightly beaten *or* 3 egg whites
2 Tbsp. honey
1 2/3 cups nonfat buttermilk

Prepare muffin tins with cooking spray. Combine cornmeal, baking soda, baking powder in a large bowl, stirring well. Add eggs, honey and buttermilk, mixing just until the dry ingredients are moistened Fill muffin tins 2/3 full. Bake. Allow muffins to cool 5 minutes before removing from tin.

Yield: 12
Oven: 350⁰F.
Time: 15 -18 minutes

CAKES

CAKES

CAKES

APPLESAUCE CAKE

1/4 cup sunflower margarine, softened
3 large eggs
1/2 cup unsweetened apple juice concentrate
1/2 cup unsweetened applesauce
1 cup unbleached flour
1 cup whole wheat flour
2 tsp. baking powder
1 tsp. baking soda
1 Tbsp. cinnamon
1/2 cup golden raisins, if desired
1 fresh cooking apple, peeled, cored and sliced thinly
Unsweetened applesauce, if desired

In bowl combine margarine, eggs, apple juice concentrate and applesauce; beat until creamy. Add flours, baking powder, baking soda, and cinnamon. Beat well. Add raisins if desired.

Grease and flour an 8" X 8" square baking pan. Line bottom of pan with apples, one layer deep. Pour batter over apples, smoothing top. Bake at 350 degrees for 25-30 minutes or until well browned. Turn onto wire rack with apple layer up to cool. Serve with warm applesauce over each piece, if desired.

Yield: 8" X 8" pan
Bake: 350^{0}F.
Time: 25-30 minutes

GRATE CARROT CAKE

1/2 cup margarine at room temperature
3 eggs
1 cup unsweetened pineapple juice
1 1/4 cup unbleached flour
1 cup whole wheat flour
1/4 cup oat bran
1 tsp. baking soda

2 tsp. baking powder
1/2 tsp. salt
1 tsp. nutmeg
2 tsp. cinnamon
3 cups finely grated carrots
1 cup unsweetened crushed pineapple juice, drained

Preheat oven. Cream eggs and butter. Stir in pineapple juice. Add flours, oat bran, baking powder, baking soda, salt, nutmeg, and cinnamon, then beat 2 minutes on medium speed with mixer. Stir in carrots and pineapple. Spray 9" X 13" pan with vegetable spray or lightly grease, then flour. Pour into pan spreading evenly. Bake 30-35 minutes until cake is lightly browned and center springs back lightly when touched. Cool on wire rack. Frost if desired with cream cheese.

Yield: 9" X 13" Cake
Bake: 350°F.
Time: 30-35 minutes

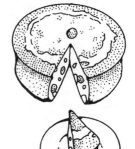

BASIC CAKE

1/4 cup sunflower margarine
2 eggs or 2 egg whites
1 tsp. vanilla
1/2 cup pineapple juice concentrate, thawed
1/2 cup unbleached flour
1/2 cup whole wheat flour
1/2 tsp. baking soda
1/2 tsp. baking powder

Spray an 8" pan with vegetable spray, then flour; set aside. Cream margarine; add eggs and vanilla, mixing well. Mix dry ingredients together. Add juice concentrate to flour mixture with electric mixer on medium speed. Beat an additional minute. Pour batter into prepared pan. Bake 20 to 25 minutes at 350°F. or until toothpick comes out clean.

Yield: 8" pan
Oven: 350°F.
Time: 20-25 minutes

ALOHA CAKE

5 eggs or egg substitute
1/3 cup safflower or canola oil
1 tsp. vanilla extract
1 tsp. almond extract
1/2 cup unsweetened pineapple juice concentrate, thawed
1 cup unsweetened apple juice concentrate, thawed
1 cup unsweetened applesauce **
1 1/2 cups crushed pineapple
2 cups unbleached flour
2 cups whole wheat flour
1/2 cup oat bran
2 tsp. baking soda
1 1/2 tsp. cinnamon

TOPPING:
1 cup crushed pineapple with juice
2/3 cup unsweetened apple juice concentrate, thawed
2 Tbsp. cornstarch
1 tsp. coconut extract

CAKE: Preheat oven. Prepare pan(s) by spraying with vegetable cooking spray. (NOTE: To facilitate removal of cake whole, line pan with waxed paper).

Combine eggs and oil and beat well. Add vanilla and almond extract, pineapple juice concentrate, applesauce and pineapple, mixing well. Combine flours, oat bran, baking soda and cinnamon, then add to egg mixture, mixing well. Then pour into pans and bake for 25-30 minutes or until lightly browned and toothpick comes out clean. Top with topping.

TOPPING: Place apple juice concentrate in 1 cup jar, then add cornstarch and shake until well-blended. Place pineapple in saucepan. Add apple juice mixture and coconut extract; cook over low heat, stirring constantly until clear and mixture thickens.

Yield: 9" X 13" or (2) 9" X 9"
Bake: 350°F.
Time: 25-30 minutes

** **Variation:** Use 1 cup ripe mashed bananas

OATMEAL CAKE

1 cup quick-cooking oats
3/4 cup boiling water
3/4 cup pineapple juice
1/2 cup honey
2 eggs *or* 3 egg whites
1/2 tsp. salt
1 tsp. baking soda
1/2 cup sunflower margarine or canola oil
1/2 cup oat bran
1/2 cup unbleached flour
1/2 cup whole wheat flour
1 tsp. vanilla
2 tsp. cinnamon

Combine oats and boiling water and let stand 5 minutes.

Prepare 9" X 13" baking pan. Cream margarine or oil to honey, juice concentrate, eggs, and vanilla. Add salt, soda, cinnamon, oat bran, flours, and oats. Blend well and turn into the prepared pan. Bake at 325°F. for 30 minutes, or until done when tested with a toothpick.

Yield: 9" X 13" pan
Oven: 325°F.
Time: 30 minutes

SPONGE CAKE

2 cups thawed apple juice concentrate
1/2 cup canola or safflower oil
1 1/2 cups whole wheat flour
1/2 cup soy flour *or* 1/2 cup more whole wheat
2 Tbsp. vanilla
6 egg yolks
6 egg whites
1/2 cup non-fat milk liquid
1 tsp. baking soda
1/2 tsp. cream of tartar

Bring apple juice and oil to a boil. Stir in whole wheat and soy flour. Remove from heat.

Heat oven to 350°F. Prepare two 8" cake pans with vegetable spray. Combine vanilla, egg yolks, milk and baking soda. Beat the egg whites and cream of tartar in small bowl until soft peaks form. Beat egg yolk mixture into flour mixture at high speed for 1 minute. Fold egg white mixture into batter, then pour into cake pans. Bake 350°F. for 30 minutes.

Yield: 2 - 8" pans
Oven: 350°F.
Time: 30 minutes

UPSIDE DOWN CAKE

FRUIT TOPPING:
2 1/2 cups chopped fruit (apples, blueberries, peaches, pine-
    apple, pears or bananas)
1 Tbsp. canola or safflower oil
2 tsp. cinnamon
1/2 tsp. nutmeg

CAKE:
1 egg
1/4 cup canola or safflower oil
5/8 cup unsweetened fruit juice concentrate (pineapple, apple
    or white grape)
1 cup unbleached flour

1/2 cup whole wheat flour
1/2 tsp. baking soda
1 tsp. baking powder

TOPPING: Toss together fruit, oil, cinnamon and nutmeg. Spoon into a greased 8" X 8" square pan.

CAKE: Combine egg, oil and juice concentrate. Beat together. Add flours, baking soda and baking powder; beat well. Pour batter over fruit, smoothing evenly. Bake at 350 degrees for 30 minutes. Cool until just warm and serve fruit side up.

Yield: 8" Sq. Pan
Oven: 350^{0}F.
Time: 30 minutes

PEAR CAKE

3/4 cup unbleached flour
1/2 cup whole wheat flour
1/2 cup date sugar
3/4 tsp. baking soda
1/8 nutmeg
1/2 cup yogurt, nonfat plain
2 egg whites
2 cups pears, peeled and chopped
1/3 cup golden raisins
TOPPING:
1 Tbsp. date sugar
1 Tbsp. walnuts or pecans, chopped

TOPPING: Combine date sugar and walnuts in small bowl. Set aside.
Combine date sugar, yogurt and raisins, set aside. Spray 8" square pan with vegetable spray. Combine the flours, baking soda, nutmeg, then add sugar mixture, mixing well to combine. Fold in pears. Spread batter evenly in pan and sprinkle topping over batter. Bake for 30 minutes or until a toothpick comes out clean. Cut to serve after cooling.

Yield: 8-9 servings
Oven: 350^{0}F.
Time: 30 minutes

APPLE COFFEE CAKE

3/4 cup unbleached flour
3/4 whole wheat flour
1/2 date sugar
1 teaspoon baking soda
3/4 tsp. cinnamon
1/2 cup apple juice concentrate
1/4 cup nonfat sour cream
1 egg white, lightly beaten
2 1/2 cups cooking apples, peeled and thinly sliced (about 3)
1/3 cup raisins

TOPPING

2 Tbsp. date sugar
2 Tbsp. walnuts, finely chopped

TOPPING: Combine date sugar and nuts in small bowl, stirring well to mix well. Set aside.

Combine apple juice, raisins and date sugar, permitting to stand a few minutes. Spray 9" pan with vegetable spray. Meanwhile, combine flours, baking soda and cinnamon in bowl, stirring to mix well. Stir in sour cream, egg white, apple juice mixture. Fold in apples. Pour into prepared pan and spread the batter evenly in pan. Sprinkle topping over batter and bake for 30 minutes or until a toothpick inserted in center comes out clean.

Yield: 8-9 servings
Oven: 350°F.
Time: 30 minutes

COOKIES

COOKIES

COOKIES

BANANA PINEAPPLE COOKIES

1 medium ripe banana, mashed (about 1/4 cup)
1/4 cup unsweetened frozen pineapple juice concentrate, thawed
1/4 cup safflower *or* canola oil
1 large egg *or* 2 egg whites
1 Tbsp. nonfat dry milk liquid
3/4 cup unbleached white flour
1/4 cup whole wheat flour
1/4 baking soda
1/2 cup flaked coconut
Grated orange rind

In a mixing bowl, beat together mashed banana, pineapple juice concentrate, oil, egg and milk until creamy. Add flours, baking soda and coconut. Beat well. Drop by rounded teaspoonfuls onto greased baking sheets and sprinkle with orange rind. Bake about 8 minutes or until just brown at 350 degrees. Cool on wire rack.

Yield: 2 dozen
Bake: 350°F.
Time: 8 minutes

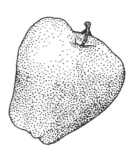

APPLESAUCE BARS

3/4 cup unbleached flour
1 cup whole wheat flour
1/4 cup oat bran
1/2 tsp. salt
1 tsp. baking soda
2 tsp. baking powder
2 tsp. cinnamon
1/2 tsp. nutmeg
1/2 cup unsweetened applesauce
1/2 cup apple juice concentrate
3 eggs *or* 4 egg whites
1/4 cup margarine
1/3 cup chopped pecans or walnuts

1/2 cup raisins

In a bowl, combine applesauce, apple juice concentrate, eggs and margarine until well blended. In separate bowl combine flours, oat bran, salt, baking soda, baking powder, cinnamon and nutmeg, then add to apple mixture, beating 2 minutes on medium speed. Stir in raisins and nuts. Spray 8" square with a vegetable-based spray. Pour mix into pan and bake until toothpick comes out clean.

Yield: 16 Bars
Oven: 350°F.
Time: 25-30 minutes

CAROB COOKIES

2 2/3 cups whole wheat flour
1/4 cup oat bran
3 Tbsp. unsweetened carob powder
2 Tbsp. baking powder
1/4 tsp. baking soda
1/2 cup + about 1/4 cup apple juice concentrate, thawed
3 Tbsp. non-fat milk
2 Tbsp. vanilla

Combine flour, carob powder, baking powder and soda in a large mixing bowl. In a smaller bowl, combine 1/2 cup apple juice, milk and vanilla. Add the liquid ingredients to the dry ones.

Beat the egg whites until soft peaks form; then work the egg whites into the dough with your hands.

Sprinkle some flour onto a board, then place dough on board, kneading 2-3 minutes. Roll dough to 1/4 inch; flour the rolling pin and board as needed. Cut into desired shapes, then place on greased baking sheets. Dip a pastry brush in the remaining 1/4 cup apple juice concentrate and brush over cookies to remove excess flour. Bake.

Yield: 4 dozen
Oven: 350°F.
Time: 20 minutes or until tops are brown

APRICOT COOKIES

1/4 cup sunflower margarine, softened
1 large egg
1/2 cup frozen unsweetened orange juice concentrate
1/2 cup frozen unsweetened apple juice concentrate
1/2 cup unbleached flour
3/4 cup whole wheat flour
1 1/4 cups rolled oats
1 tsp. baking soda
1/2 cup dried apricots, chopped
1/2 cup dates, chopped
1/2 cup golden raisins
1/4 cup pecans or walnuts, chopped, if desired

In mixing bowl combine margarine, egg, orange and apple juice concentrates. Beat well. Add flours, rolled oats and baking soda, mixing until smooth. Stir in apricots, dates, raisins, and nuts if desired. Drop by teaspoonful onto greased cookie sheet. Bake at 350 degrees for 12 minutes, or until slightly brown.

Yield: 3 dozen
Oven: 350°F.
Time: 12 minutes

BROWNIE OATMEALS

1/2 cup very ripe mashed banana (about 1 large)
1/3 cup safflower oil
1/4 tsp. vanilla extract
2 eggs
1/4 cup nonfat dry milk liquid
1/2 cup whole wheat flour
3/4 cup unbleached flour
1/4 cup carob powder
1/4 tsp. baking soda
2/3 cup rolled oats
1 cup chopped walnuts or pecans

Mash banana. In medium mixing bowl beat together mashed banana, oil, vanilla extract, eggs, and milk until creamy. Add flours, carob powder, and baking soda. Beat well. Stir in oats and chopped nuts; mix well. Grease cookie sheets. Drop by teaspoonfuls onto cookie sheets. Bake at 350 degrees for 8-10 minutes or until just firm to the touch. Cool on wire racks.

Yield: 4 dozen
Oven: 350°F.
Time: 8-10 minutes

TEA COOKIES

2 1/2 cups whole wheat flour
1/8 tsp. salt
1 1/2 tsp. baking powder
1/2 cup margarine
1/4 cup apple, white grape *or* pineapple juice concentrate
   thawed
1 tsp. vanilla
2 tsp. honey

Sift dry ingredients together. Cream the margarine; then add juice concentrate, vanilla, and honey. Combine the dry ingredients with the juice mixture.

Knead the dough into a ball, adding the remainder of the apple juice as needed to achieve a firm texture; then chill the dough for 1 hour. Then roll the dough into 3/4 inch thick and cut into desired shapes with knife, glass or cookie cutter. Place on greased cookie sheet and bake.

Yield: 3 1/2 dozen
Oven: 325°F.
Time: 5 minutes

VARIATIONS:
1) Add 1/2 cup almonds, raisins, poppy seeds, or coconut.
2) Substitute orange juice for apple juice.

CAROB NUT BROWNIES

1/3 cup margarine
1/2 cup carob chips
1/4 cup honey
1 egg
15 pkgs. Equal*
1 tsp. vanilla
1/2 cup oat bran, uncooked
1/3 cup whole wheat flour
1/2 cup chopped nuts

Grease 8 inch pan lightly with oil. In medium saucepan, melt margarine and carob chips over medium heat, stirring constantly or in bowl, melt carob chips and margarine in microwave using warm setting. Cool. Add honey, egg and vanilla; mix well. Add flour and 1/4 cup nuts. Spread into prepared pan; sprinkle with remaining nuts. Bake. Cool, then cut into squares.

Yield: 16
Oven: 350⁰F.
Time: 16 minutes for chewy brownie
18 minutes for cakelike brownie

* **Substitute** for Equal: 1/4 cup pineapple juice concentrate. Increase flour to 2/3 cup.

RAISIN APPLE BARS

1/2 cup unsweetened applesauce
1/2 cup frozen unsweetened apple juice concentrate, thawed
3 eggs
1/4 cup sunflower margarine, softened
1 cup unbleached flour
1 cup whole wheat flour
1 tsp. baking soda
2 tsp. baking powder
1 tsp. nutmeg
3 tsp. cinnamon

1 cup raisins
Cinnamon for topping

In mixing bowl mix eggs and butter until well blended. Add applesauce and juice concentrate, mixing well. Beat in flours, baking soda, baking powder, cinnamon, and nutmeg. Stir in raisins. Pour batter into a greased and floured 8" X 8" square pan. Sprinkle with additional cinnamon. Bake 25 minutes at 350 degrees until a toothpick inserted comes out clean. Cool.

Yield: 8" X 8" pan
Oven: 350⁰F.
Time: 25 minutes

OATMEAL COOKIES

1/4 cup honey
1/2 cup sunflower margarine *or* Crisco
1 egg, slightly beaten
2 tsp. vanilla
1/2 tsp. salt
1/2 cup whole wheat flour
3/4 tsp. baking powder
1 cup wheat germ *or* fortified flax
1 1/2 cup rolled oats
3/4 cup raisins
3/4 cup nuts or sunflower seeds

Heat oven. Cream margarine and honey. Add egg, vanilla, salt, then blend. Mix flour, baking powder, wheat germ, rolled oats with fork to blend; then add to honey-egg margarine mixture. Add remaining ingredients. A few drops of water may be added to make dough proper consistency. Spoon onto greased cookie sheets and flatten slightly with spoon. Bake.

Yield: 3 dozen
Oven: 375⁰F.
Time: 8-10 minutes

ORANGE COOKIES

4 large eggs
1/2 cup safflower oil
6 ounce can frozen unsweetened orange juice concentrate
1/3 cup orange juice
2 cups unbleached flour
1/2 tsp. baking powder
Grated orange rind

In a mixing bowl beat together eggs, oil, orange juice concentrate, and orange juice. Add flour and baking powder, and
beat well. Drop mix by teaspoonful onto greased cookie
sheet. Sprinkle grated orange rind over each cookie. Bake at
375⁰F. for 8 minutes or until cookies are slightly raised and
firm to touch. (Be careful not to overcook as bottoms will
burn.) Carefully remove from baking pans and place on wire
racks to cool.

VARIATION: Lemon Sours--Prepare as above, except use
frozen pineapple juice concentrate and lemon juice in place
of orange. Top with grated lemon rind.

Yield: 5 dozen
Oven: 375⁰F.
Time: 8 minutes

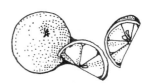

SQUASH COOKIES

1/3 cup canola or safflower oil
1 large egg *or* 2 egg whites
1 cup squash, cooked, drained and mashed
3/4 cup unbleached flour
3/4 cup whole wheat flour
1/2 tsp. baking powder
1 tsp. nutmeg
1 tsp. cinnamon
1 1/2 cups finely chopped dates
Walnut or pecan pieces

Mix together oil, egg, and squash. Add flours, baking powder, and spices and mix well. Stir in chopped dates. Drop

batter by small teaspoonfuls onto greased cookie sheet. Top each cookie with a nut piece. Bake at 350 degrees for 10 minutes or until firm to the touch. Cool on wire rack.

Yield: 3 dozen
Oven: 350°F.
Time: 10 minutes

FILLED OATMEAL COOKIES

3 cups oats
1/2 cup tahini
1 Tbsp. canola *or* sunflower oil
1/2 tsp. salt
Flour--oat, rice or wheat
1 cup distilled water

Mix oats, tahini, oil and salt. Add water then add enough flour until mixture holds together. Roll out until about 1/4 inch thick and cut circles.

3/4 cup raisins or dried apples or mixed dry fruit
1 cup distilled water
1/8 tsp. salt

Combine ingredients in saucepan. Bring to a boil, then simmer 10-15 minutes. Puree. Cook until thick. Spoon onto 1 circle of dough and cover with another circle. (*Alternative way*--spoon filling in center and fold 1 circle in half and seal.) Seal edges with a wet fork. Bake at 375°F. until brown about 35-45 minutes.

Yield: 1 dozen
Oven: 375°F.
Time: 35-40 minutes

SUGAR"LESS" COOKIES

1 cup raisins
3/4 cup dates, minced
1 cup cooking apples, peeled, cored and chopped
1 cup frozen unsweetened apple juice concentrate
1/4 cup sunflower margarine, softened
2 eggs
1 tsp. vanilla
1 cup unbleached flour
1 cup whole wheat flour
1 tsp. soda
1 cup rolled oats
1/2 cup chopped nuts, if desired

Combine raisins, dates, apples, and apple juice concentrate. Bring to a boil for 10 minutes. Add butter to mixture while hot; then place in mixing bowl and let cool. Then add eggs and vanilla; beat well. Beat in flours, soda and oats, mixing well. Stir in nuts, if desired. Spray cookie sheet with vegetable spray. Drop by teaspoonful onto cookie sheet. Bake at 350⁰F. for 12 minutes or until golden brown.

Yield: 4 dozen
Oven: 350⁰F.
Time: 12 minutes

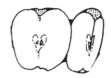

APPLE COOKIES

4 large eggs *or* egg substitute
1/2 cup safflower *or* canola oil
6 ounce can frozen unsweetened pineapple juice concentrate, thawed
1/3 cup lemon juice
2 cups unbleached flour
1/2 tsp. baking powder
Cinnamon

Beat together eggs, oil, pineapple juice concentrate and lemon juice in mixing bowl. Add flour and baking powder, beat well. Drop mix by teaspoonful onto greased baking sheet. Sprinkle cinnamon over each cookie. Bake at 375 degrees for 8 minutes or until cookies are firm to touch. (Be careful not to overcook as bottoms will burn.) Carefully remove from baking pans and allow to cool.

Yield: 5 dozen
Oven: 375°F.
Time: 8 minutes

WHEATLESS OATMEAL COOKIES

1 to 1 1/2 cups oatmeal
1/4 tsp. salt
1 Tbsp. canola *or* sunflower oil
1 to 1 1/2 cups distilled water *or* apple or pineapple juice
Raisins, if desired
Chopped nuts, if desired
Sesame seeds, if desired

Mix oatmeal, salt, oil, and water and set aside for 10 minutes until oatmeal is soft and the water is absorbed. Add raisins, nuts, or sesame seeds, if desired. Drop on greased cookie sheet and press out. Bake for 30-45 minutes until brown and dry. Remove from cookie sheet and allow to cool.

Yield: 18-24
Oven: 375°F.
Time: 30-45 minutes

QUICK WALNUT COOKIES

3 egg whites
1/4 tsp. cream of tartar
2 Tbsp. white grape *or* apple juice concentrate
1/8 tsp. cinnamon
1 1/2 cups walnuts, very finely chopped

Beat egg whites until foamy and soft peaks. Add cream of tartar beating until egg whites are stiff. Mix in juice concentrate. Add cinnamon; then fold in nuts. Drop by teaspoonfuls on cookie sheet. Bake at 325°F. for 10-15 minutes until lightly browned. Cool.

Yield: 3 dozen
Oven: 325°F.
Time: 10-15 minutes

BANANA COOKIES

3 cups rolled oats
1/2 tsp. salt
1 1/2 tsp. cinnamon
1/4 cup canola or safflower oil
3/4 cup walnuts, chopped
1 3/4 cup very ripe mashed bananas (about 4 medium)

Mix oats, salt and cinnamon. Add oil and toss to coat; reserve. Mash very ripe bananas with fork or food processor. Add nuts and bananas to oat mixture, then mix well. Spoon by heaping tablespoon onto ungreased cookie sheet. Flatten cookies with fork or spatula. Bake at 400 degrees on high rack for 10 minutes; remove from oven and press each cookie flatter with fork. Return cookies to oven and continue baking another 8-10 minutes.

Yield: 24
Oven: 400°F.
Time: 10 then 8 minutes

DESSERTS

DESSERTS

DESSERTS

BANANA DREAM FLOAT

4 medium bananas, sliced
1/8 tsp. nutmeg
1/4 tsp. cinnamon
10 pkg. Equal and 1/2 cup plain yogurt *or*
  1/2 cup fruit juice sweetened yogurt without sugar

Mix nutmeg, cinnamon and Equal. Fold in sliced bananas.
Chill for 30 to 45 minutes, then serve.

Yield: 4 servings
Chill

BERRY PUDDING

2 cups "Berry" juice (frozen unsweetened juice can be used)
2 Tbsp. agar flakes*
1 cup fresh pineapple, chopped

Add agar flakes to juice and bring to a boil, then simmer 2-3
minutes until agar is melted. Allow to cool about 10 minutes, then gently mix in pineapple. Place in refrigerator to
set. Ready to eat in about 30 minutes.

* Agar is made from red algae, and is actually a vegetable. Agar
flakes may be used in place of gelatin. In fact, when using high-
acid fruits like pineapple, agar is preferable. Agar flakes can be
found in health food stores. Basic substitution is 2 Tbsp. agar to 2
cups liquid. Add flakes to liquid, bring to a boil and simmer 2-3
minutes, stirring until agar is melted. Cool to thicken.

Yield: 2 servings
Chill

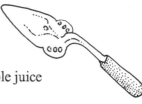

MARGARITA CHEESECAKE

12 oz. can frozen unsweetened pineapple juice
1 Tbsp. gelatin
4 ounces Tofu
8 ounces low-fat ricotta cheese *or* 8 ounces cottage cheese
2 Tbsp crushed ice
12 tablets Equal

1 tsp. vanilla
1/4 tsp. grated lemon peel
1 Tbsp. lime juice

Dissolve gelatin in 1/4 cup cold water, then set aside. Bring pineapple juice to boil over high heat, simmer down to 6 ounces. Add dissolved gelatin to pineapple juice. Stir until dissolved. Pour all remaining ingredients in blender or food processor, add pineapple mixture, then blend until smooth. Pour into shallow dish (9 x 5 x 3 inches). Chill until set.

Yield: 9" X 5" dish
Chill

BLUEBERRY CHEESECAKE

1 pound low fat cottage cheese
1 egg white
1/2 cup plain low fat yogurt
1 tsp. vanilla
2 tsp. lemon juice
1/4 cup frozen orange juice concentrate
2 ripe bananas, cut up
3 Tbsp. unbleached flour

TOPPING:

8 oz. can undrained crushed pineapple
1/4 cup frozen orange juice concentrate
1 Tbsp. arrowroot
1 cup fresh or frozen blueberries

In food processor, blend together cheese, egg white, yogurt and lemon juice; mix thoroughly. Add fruit juice concentrate, bananas and flour. Continue blending (about 3 minutes) until mixture is creamy. Pour into a non-stick 9 inch pie pan and bake. Cool.

For topping, combine all ingredients in a small saucepan. Cook over medium heat stirring constantly until sauce thickens. Cool and pour over the cheesecake.

Yield: 9" pie

DATE-RICE PUDDING

1 cup "quick" brown rice
1 1/2 cups water
1/4 tsp. salt, if desired
1/2 cup milk or soymilk
1 tsp. vanilla
1 cup pitted dates
1 Tbsp. arrowroot powder or cornstarch

Cook rice in water and salt for 12 minutes. Blend remaining ingredients in food processor, blending well, then pour into a saucepan. Stir over low-medium heat until mixture is thick. Stir in rice, and let stand 5 minutes before serving. Spoon into individual dishes and sprinkle with cinnamon.

NOTE: 1 1/2 cups cooked brown rice can be substituted for quick brown rice, water, and salt.

Yield: 3 servings

FRUITY GELLO

12 ounce can unsweetened fruit juice concentrate
1 1/4 cups water
2 Tbsp. unflavored gelatin or 2 envelopes gelatin

Measure 1/2 cup of water and sprinkle gelatin over it. Let soak at least 5 minutes to soften, set aside. Pour juice concentrate into saucepan. Bring to a boil; add gelatin, stirring until dissolved. Remove from heat; add remaining water. Pour into 9" X 13" pan or into individual cups. Refrigerate until set. Serve as desired.

Yield: 9" X 13" pan

VARIATIONS:
1) Add 2 cups sliced bananas after gello just begins to gel. Then chill until firm.
2) Add 2 cups fresh sliced strawberries. Chill until firm.
3) Using an 8 ounce can crushed pineapple, separate juice from pineapple, reserve. Add enough water to make 1 1/4 cup water / juice and substitute for water in above recipe. Add pineapple to gello when gello just begins to gel. Chill until set.

FRUITY SHAKE

6 ounces frozen unsweetened fruit juice concentrate (apple, orange, pineapple *or* cranberry)
4 cups very cold nonfat dry milk, reconstituted liquid
Cinnamon or nutmeg

Chill glasses in freezer about 30 minutes prior to mixing recipe. Using food processor, whip fruit juice concentrate and 2 cups of milk until frothy. Add remainder of milk and mix thoroughly. Pour into chilled glasses and sprinkle with dash of cinnamon or nutmeg.

Yield: 6 servings

FRUITY YOGURT "CREAM"

1 Tbsp. lemon juice
2 Tbsp. pineapple juice or water
1 Tbsp. gelatin
1 cup fresh fruit, cut in pieces
8 oz. can crushed pineapple in its own juice, drained
8 oz. cup plain low fat yogurt

In a small pan, combine lemon juice and pineapple juice or water. Add gelatin, then set aside for 5 minutes. Then stir mixture over low heat until gelatin dissolves. Remove from heat and add fruits and yogurt. Beat with electric mixer until fluffy. Freeze until firm.

Yield: 4 servings
Freeze

FRUITY YOGURT POPSICLES

2 cups plain or vanilla yogurt
1 cup fruit juice--orange, grape, pineapple, etc.
4 pkg. Equal (optional)
2 tsp. vanilla

Whip in food processor or blender until well mixed. Freeze in popsicle molds, ice trays or paper cups with stick.

Yield: 6 servings

SWEET RICE PUDDING

8 oz. can crushed pineapple + water
1 cup glutinous brown rice *
3 large eggs, well beaten
3 cups non-fat dry milk liquid
1/2 cup powdered nonfat dry milk
1/2 tsp. nutmeg
1 tsp. cinnamon
1/2 tsp. ginger
1/2 cup golden raisins

Separate pineapple and juice, reserving both. Combine pineapple juice with enough water to make 2 cups of liquid. Combine this liquid with rice in saucepan with tightly fitting cover, then cook until rice is tender (45-50 minutes). Allow rice to cool 10 minutes. Meanwhile, combine pineapple with remaining ingredients in large mixing bowl. Add 1/2 cup of rice at a time, mixing well until all rice is added. Pour mixture into 2 quart oven dish. Bake at 350 degrees for 50 minutes, stirring twice. Remove from oven, stirring again. Allow pudding to cool at least 30 minutes before serving. Serve warm or cooled as desired.

* **NOTE:** Most glutinous or sweet brown rice is short-grained. Despite its name, it contains no gluten. It is high in protein, easily digested, moister and very sticky when cooked. For an easy dessert, combine cooked glutinous rice with a little milk, dash of cinnamon or nutmeg and dried fruit.

Yield: 10 servings
Oven: 325°F.
Time: 25 minutes

QUICK FROZEN PINEAPPLE DELIGHT

8 ounce can unsweetened crushed pineapple in its own juice

Place can of crushed pineapple in the freezer and allow to freeze. Remove the pineapple by opening both ends of the can and pushing the frozen pineapple out into a blender or food processor. Blend at high speed until creamy. Pour the pineapple into serving dishes and refreeze to desired consistency.
Yield: 3 servings

CRUSTLESS PUMPKIN MOUSSE

2 eggs, separated
1 cup apple juice concentrate, thawed
16 oz. can pumpkin
2 tsp. cinnamon
3/4 tsp. ginger
1/4 tsp. cloves
1 Tbsp. *or* 1 envelope unflavored gelatin
1/4 cup water

Allow gelatin to soak in water. In a saucepan, beat egg yolks and apple juice concentrate with wire whip. Add pumpkin, cinnamon, ginger and cloves, stir. Cook over medium heat, stirring constantly until mixture thickens. Remove from heat. Add dissolved gelatin into warm pumpkin mixture. Refrigerate until partially set. Beat egg whites until stiff, then fold into pumpkin mixture until well-blended. Spoon into individual serving dishes and refrigerate until serving time. If desired, garnish with whipped cream.

Yield: 6 servings
Chill

BROWN RICE PUDDING

3 eggs or egg substitute
3/4 cup thawed, unsweetened apple juice concentrate
1/2 tsp vanilla
1 cup non-fat dry milk, reconstituted
1 1/2 cups cooked brown rice
1/4-1/2 cup raisins

Beat eggs, add apple juice concentrate and vanilla. Beat well. Stir in milk and blend well. Add rice and raisins. Spray 1 1/2 quart baking dish with vegetable spray, then pour rice mixture into it. Bake.

Yield: 6 servings
Bake: 350⁰F.
Time: 40 minutes

CREAMY RICE PUDDING

1 cup whipped cream
1/2 tsp. vanilla extract
16 oz. can crushed pineapple, drained
2 cups brown rice
Dash cinnamon
Dash nutmeg, if desired

Make sure pineapple is well drained or cream will separate. Save pineapple juice to drink or for other recipes. Fold together whipped cream, vanilla, and pineapple in large bowl. Add rice slowly, mixing together. Spoon into individual serving dishes and sprinkle with cinnamon and/or nutmeg, if desired. Refrigerate about an hour before serving.

Yield: 6 Servings

STRAWBERRY MOUSSE

4 1/2 Tbsp. plain gelatin
1 cup unsweetened apple juice concentrate
1 cup plain nonfat yogurt
1 cup strawberries, pureed
2 cups sliced strawberries

Soften gelatin in apple juice concentrate for 5 minutes. Bring to a boil, stirring constantly, until gelatin is dissolved. Allow to cool, then add pureed strawberries to gelatin, mixing well. Refrigerate until mixture begins to thicken slightly, then add yogurt, whipping until light and foaming. Fold in sliced strawberries, then pour into serving bowl.

Yield: 10 servings

CRISP APPLE PUDDING

CRUST
1 cup rolled oats
1/2 cup unbleached flour
1/2 cup whole wheat flour

1/2 cup Grape Nuts cereal
1 tsp. cinnamon
1 cup apple juice

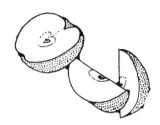

FILLING

2 cups sliced apples
1/2 cup raisins
1-2 tsp. cinnamon
1 Tbsp. lemon juice
2 tsp. arrowroot

To make crust, combine dry ingredients. Stir in apple juice until mixture holds together. Divide in two and press half in the bottom and up the sides of a non-stick 9" pie pan; reserve remaining crust mixture for topping. Bake bottom crust for 5 minutes.

To make filling, combine all ingredients in medium-sized saucepan. Bring to a boil over medium heat and simmer for 10 minutes until apples are slightly tender. Remove apples and raisins with a slotted spoon and place in pie shell. Increase heat and continue cooking sauce until it thickens. Pour sauce over apples and raisins. For a topping, crumble remaining crust over filling. Bake 30 minutes at 375°F.

Yield: 6 to 8 servings
Oven: 375°F.
Time: 30 minutes

FRUITY GELLO SQUARES

12 oz. can unsweetened fruit juice concentrate
2 1/2 cups water
4 Tbsp. or envelopes unflavored gelatin

Take 1 cup of water and sprinkle gelatin over it; let stand for 5 minutes to soften. Add the juice concentrate to the remainder of the water in pan, bring to a boil; then pour into the gelatin mixture, stirring until dissolved. Pour into 9" X 13" pan. Refrigerate until firm. Cut into 2" squares.

Yield: 48 2" Squares

FRUIT FREEZE

1 large banana
12 strawberries, washed, with stem removed
2-3 ounces orange juice concentrate

Peel banana, then wrap in plastic wrap. Wrap strawberries in plastic wrap. Freeze both until frozen.

Grate banana and strawberries in a food processor. Add 2-3 ounces of orange juice concentrate (frozen) and then 1/3 to 1/2 cup of water, blending to a smooth mixture. Serve in a dessert glass. Garnish with fresh strawberry or piece of mint.

Yield: 3 servings
Serve immediately.

VARIATIONS: Pears, grapes, or peaches for fruits and apple, grape, pineapple juice.

BLUEBERRY SUPREME

2 Tbsp. unflavored gelatin
1/2 cup cold pineapple juice
2 sticks cinnamon
3 cups pineapple juice
1 Tbsp. lemon juice
1 cup crushed pineapple in its own juice, drained
1 cup fresh or frozen blueberries

Soften gelatin in 1/2 cup cold pineapple juice. In a medium sized pan, combine the remaining pineapple juice and the cinnamon sticks. Bring to a boil and simmer for 5 minutes. Remove cinnamon sticks and blend in the softened gelatin.

Chill until the mixture begins to thicken. Fold in the pineapple, lemon juice, and the blueberries. Pour into a 4 cup mold and chill until firm.

For extra attractiveness when serving, place low fat cottage cheese around the edges and garnish with fresh mint.

Yield: 6 servings

SUGAR FREE FRUIT GELLO

1 cup water
1 cup orange juice
1 Tbsp. gelatin or 1 envelope
1 cup fresh fruits *or* 1/2 cup canned crushed pineapple, if
    desired

Combine all ingredients except fruit in medium-sized pan;
set aside for 5 minutes. Then cook over low heat, stirring until gelatin dissolves. Cool. Pour into a dish, chill in refrigerator. As gelatin starts to thicken, add fruit if desired.

Yield: 4-6 servings
Time: 2 hours chill time

NOTE: Commercial presweetened regular gelatin is 88% sugar.
Gelatin made from fresh fruits and fruit juices can be just as sweet.

APPLE BREAD PUDDING

3 large eggs or egg substitute
12 oz. can skimmed evaporated milk *or*
    1 cup nonfat dry milk, reconstituted
3/4 cup apple juice concentrate, thawed
1 tsp. vanilla
1 large cooking apple, peeled, cored and grated
4 slices whole wheat bread with crust removed
1/2 to 3/4 cup raisins
Cinnamon

Cut bread into 16 squares per slice, then set aside. Beat eggs,
then add apple juice concentrate. In a double boiler, scald
milk until scum forms. Slowly add milk to egg mixture.
Add vanilla and apple. Spray 1 1/2 quart baking dish with
vegetable spray, then pour egg mixture into dish. Press bread
and raisins into egg mixture. Lightly sprinkle cinnamon over
top. Bake until custard is thick and bread is lightly browned.

Yield: 8 servings
Oven: 350^{0}F.
Time: 45 minutes

QUICK PINEAPPLE ICE

1 egg white
2 Tbsp. orange or pineapple juice
1 Tbsp. orange juice rind, grated
2 (8 oz.) cans crushed pineapple in its own juice

In a large bowl, mix all ingredients together. Then place in the freezer until slightly frozen. Remove and beat with an electric mixer until fluffy. Pour into serving dishes and return to the freezer for 45 minutes. Serve when almost firm, but not too hard for best flavor. If it is too hard or if you wish to make it in advance, allow it to soften in the refrigerator 30 to 40 minutes before serving.

Yield: 4 servings
Serve Immediately

FROZEN STRAWBERRY DELIGHT

4 cups fresh strawberries, cleaned, hulled, then frozen
1/4 cup unsweetened apple juice concentrate, thawed

Freeze cleaned strawberries on tray in single layer. In food processor, grate frozen strawberries. Unplug processor to change to whipping blade; gradually add apple juice whipping until smooth. Pour into serving dishes and serve immediately. Garnish with fresh strawberry.

Yield: 4 Servings

VARIATION: Try unsweetened orange, white grape juice or other unsweetened juice concentrate.

APPLES 'N FIGS

4 cooking apples
1 tsp. cinnamon
1 lemon
1/2 cup chopped dried figs
1/4 cup orange juice, divided

Prepare apples by coring and peeling 1/3 of the way down.

Grate lemon peel, reserve. Mix cinnamon, lemon peel and chopped figs with 2 Tbsp. (1/2) of orange juice. Stuff apples with mixture using small spoon. Place apples in glass baking dish. Spoon remainder of juice over apples. Cover with plastic wrap. Then microwave on high for 8 minutes or until tender as cooking time may vary depending on the variety and size of the apples. Let stand 3 minutes before removing from oven. Serve either warm or chilled as desired.

Yield: 4 servings
Microwave: 8 minutes

TAPIOCA PUDDING

3 Tbsp. quick-cooking tapioca

1 egg, separated

2 1/4 cup nonfat dry milk, reconstituted

3/4 cup unsweetened apple juice concentrate, thawed (Save 1 tsp.)

1 tsp. vanilla

Combine tapioca, egg yolk and apple juice concentrate in a saucepan. Slowly add milk, stirring to blend well. Let stand 5 minutes. Beat egg white until foamy; gradually beat in 1 teaspoon apple juice, beating to soft peaks. Set aside. Cook tapioca mixture over medium heat to a full boil, stirring constantly. Remove from heat. Gradually add to beaten egg white, stirring quickly to blend. Stir in vanilla extract, then pour into individual dishes or 1 large bowl.

Yield: 6 servings

CHUNKY APPLESAUCE

4 pounds (14-16) cooking apples

1/2 cup apple juice concentrate, thawed

Dash cinnamon

Peel and remove seeds from apples, then cut into 1/2 inch pieces. Combine apples and apple juice concentrate in a 3 quart saucepan. Cover and cook over medium-low heat, about 30 minutes or until apples are soft, stirring at intervals. Mash the apples to desired consistency with potato masher. Serve with dash of cinnamon.

Yield: 6-8

PEACH COBBLER

FILLING

1/4 cup date sugar
1/2 cup orange juice
2 Tbsp. cornstarch
1/2 tsp. cinnamon
1/8 tsp. nutmeg
4 1/2-5 cups peaches, sliced (about 5 medium)

BATTER

1 cup unbleached flour
1/3 cup oatmeal, uncooked
1/3 cup date sugar
1 1/2 tsp. baking powder
1/2 tsp. baking soda
1/8 tsp. cinnamon
3/4 cup nonfat buttermilk

Filling: Spray 2 quart dish with vegetable spray. Combine orange juice, date sugar, cornstarch, cinnamon and nutmeg in 2 quart saucepan, mixing well. Heat over medium heat, stirring constantly for 5 minutes or until mixture thickens and bubbles. Remove from heat. Stir in peaches, coating well. Pour into prepared glass dish.

Batter: Combine dry ingredients in a bowl. Stir in buttermilk. Pour batter evenly over peaches. Bake until top is golden brown and bubbles appear around edges. If top browns too quickly, cover with foil. Allow to cool 15 minutes before serving.

Yield: 8
Oven: 350⁰F.
Time: 40 minutes

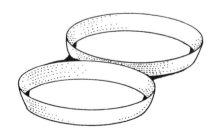

SWEET POTATO PUDDING

1 cup sweet potato, cooked and mashed *or* pumpkin
3 eggs *or* 4 egg whites
2/3 cup honey *or* maple syrup
1 1/2 tsp. cinnamon
1/2 tsp. ginger
1/4 tsp. nutmeg
dash cloves
2 cans (12 ounce) evaporated skim milk
1/2 cup whole grain cornmeal

Cook sweet potatoes until soft. Mash. Spray 2 quart baking dish with vegetable spray. Combine sweet potato, eggs, honey and spices in a food processor and blend until smooth. Set aside.

Combine cornmeal and milk in 2 quart saucepan, stirring to mix well. Cook over medium heat about 15 minutes, stirring constantly until mixture thickens and is bubbly. Reduce heat to low. Add about half of the cornmeal mixture to sweet potato mixture, blending to mix well. Then pour all of sweet potato mixture into the cornmeal mixture. Continue to cook for 3 minutes or until mixture thickens slightly. Pour into baking dish. Place dish in a pan filled with 1 inch hot water. Bake until a sharp knife inserted midway between center of pudding and edge of dish comes out clean. Allow to cool for 30 minutes before serving.

Yield: 8 servings
Oven: 350⁰F.
Time: 90 minutes

FLUFFY APRICOT DELIGHT

1 cup dried apricots
2 cups water
1/3 cup honey
2 Tbsp. lemon juice
1 tsp. almond *or* vanilla extract
4 egg whites

Combine apricots and water in saucepan. Bring to a boil and simmer for 15 minutes or until apricots are soft. Then pour into food processor. Add lemon juice, honey and extract, blending until smooth. Cool in large bowl.

Beat egg whites until stiff with mixer. Fold gently into mixture with a rubber spatula. Spoon into serving bowl or individual glasses. Chill for 3 hours before serving.

Yield: 6 servings
Chill

PIES N' PASTRY

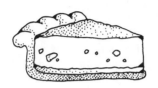

PIES N' PASTRY

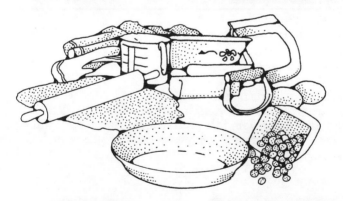

PIES N' PASTRY

CRUSTS

LOW CHOLESTEROL PIE CRUST

2 cups whole wheat flour *or*
   1 cup unbleached flour and 1 cup whole wheat flour
1/2 cup canola or safflower oil
1/2 tsp. salt, if desired
4-6 Tbsp. ice water

Mix flour and salt then add oil, mixing well with a fork. Add water to get desired consistency. Roll out dough on a lightly floured surface or roll between 2 pieces of plastic wrap. Place in pan. Fill as desired.

Yield: 2 9" or 10" crusts

EASY PIE CRUST

1 1/2 cups unbleached flour
1 1/2 cups whole wheat flour
1 tsp. baking powder
1/2 tsp. salt, if desired
8 ounces Crisco shortening
1/2 cup boiling water

Mix water and shortening together, then set aside. Mix dry ingredients together; make well in bowl. Add water shortening mixture, mixing with fork until dough forms ball. Chill, if desired. Roll out between two pieces of plastic wrap. Bake as desired.

Yield: 4 10" crusts

MERINGUE SHELLS

4 egg whites
1/2 tsp. cream of tartar
1 tsp. apple *or* white grape juice concentrate, thawed
1/2 tsp. vanilla extract

Preheat oven. Beat egg whites until foamy and soft peaks form; add cream of tartar, beating until very stiff--DO NOT underbeat. Continue beating and slowly add apple juice and vanilla; beat until well-blended. Divide into 6 mounds on lightly greased cookie sheet; shape into 4 to 5 inch diameter shells with deep crevice in center. Bake about 45 minutes until lightly browned and firm to touch. Remove from pan and cool on wire rack. Fill just before serving with slice fruit or sugar-free pudding.

Yield: 6
Oven: 275°F.
Time: 45 minutes

PAT-A-PIE CRUST

1/2 cup flour
1/2 cup whole wheat flour
1/4 tsp. salt, if desired
1/3 cup sunflower, canola *or* corn oil
1 1/2 Tbsp. non-fat instant milk liquid

Combine flours and salt. Mix oil and milk together, then add to flour mixture all at once. Stir only until dough forms a ball. Pat into a 9" pie pan.

Yield: 9" pie crust

BANANA CUSTARD PIE

1 Tbsp. whole wheat flour
dash salt
3 egg yolks, slightly beaten
2 cups scaled non-fat dry milk liquid
1 tsp. vanilla
1 large banana, sliced
8 pkg. Equal

Mix flour, salt and egg yolks in top of double boiler. Slowly add milk. Then add vanilla and cook about 15 minutes over medium heat until mixture thickens, stirring occasionally. Cover bottom of 9" baked pie shell with banana slices. Remove custard from heat and allow to cool slightly, then add Equal. Pour into pie shell and garnish with bananas that have been dipped in 1/8 tsp. ascorbic acid crystals mixed with 1 ounce of water.

Yield: 9" pie

PUMPKIN PIE FILLING

3 eggs
16 oz. can pumpkin
3/4 cup apple juice concentrate, thawed
1/4 tsp. salt
1 Tbsp. cinnamon
1 tsp. ginger
1/2 tsp. nutmeg
1/4 tsp. cloves
1 (12 ounce) skimmed evaporated milk *or*
  2 scoops Tofu milk powder mixed with 12 ounces of water

In large bowl mix eggs well. Beat in pumpkin, mixing well. Then add apple juice concentrate, then salt and spices, blending well. Slowly add evaporated or tofu milk, stirring to blend. Pour into an unbaked pie crust. Bake 15 minutes at 475^{0}F.; then without opening oven door, reduce oven temperature to 375^{0}F., continuing to bake an additional 40-45 minutes or until kitchen knife inserted in the center comes out clean. (See note next page.)

NOTE: Center may be slightly soft.

Yield: 9"-10" pie
Oven: 475°F./ 375°F.
Time: 15 minutes / 40-45 minutes

APPLE CRISP

Juice of 1 lemon
2 cups water
4 large cooking apples (about 2 pounds)
1/2 cup unsweetened apple juice concentrate, thawed
1 tsp. grated lemon peel
1 tsp. cinnamon
1/4 tsp. ground ginger

TOPPING:

1/2 cup rolled oats
1/4 cup flour
1 tsp. cinnamon
2 Tbsp. honey
2 Tbsp. margarine

Heat oven to 375°F. Spray 9 inch square glass baking dish with vegetable spray. Place lemon juice and water in a bowl. Peel, core and thinly slice apples then drop into lemon water to prevent browning. In another bowl mix apple juice, lemon peel, cinnamon, ginger and 1/4 cup of the lemon water, then toss in apples and spoon into baking dish. Cook in microwave (700 watts) on High for 7 minutes or until apples are tender but not mushy, stirring twice. Remove from microwave.

For topping, combine dry ingredients in a bowl. Add honey. Cut in margarine, tossing lightly with fingers until mixture resembles coarse meal. Sprinkle topping evenly over apples and bake until bubbly and golden about 18-20 minutes. Allow to cool for 5 minutes before serving.

Yield: 9" dish
Oven: 375°F.
Time: 20 minutes

APPLE FILLING

3 pounds* Granny Smith *or* other cooking apples, peeled, sliced into 1/4 inch pieces
1/2 cup raisins
1 cup frozen apple juice concentrate, thawed
4 tsp. tapioca, cornstarch *or* flour
1 tsp. lemon juice, optional 1 Tbsp cinnamon
1/4 tsp. nutmeg

Mix apples, raisins, apple juice concentrate, cinnamon, nutmeg, tapioca and stir until apples are well coated. Add lemon juice, if desired, to keep apples lighter-colored. Pour into prepared unbaked pie crust pan and top with the second crust. Seal edges and cut slits in the top crust to allow steam to escape. Bake until golden brown.

APPLE PIE

CRUST:
2/3 cup whole wheat flour
2/3 cup unbleached flour
1/2 cup oat bran
1/2 tsp. salt *or* salt substitute
2/3 cup vegetable shortening *or* margarine
1 egg *or* egg white
4-5 Tbsp. cold water

Combine flours, oat bran, salt and butter *or* shortening (can use food processor or mixer) to coarse meal. Combine egg, water and vinegar, then add to flour mixture. mixing until all ingredients are moistened. Divide dough in two, wrap in plastic wrap, then chill 1 hour.

Lightly flour pastry cloth or using 2 overlapping pieces of plastic wrap on counter, place crust in middle of one sheet, cover with another piece of wrap, then roll into 14" circle. Carefully remove upper wrap, then gently lift into 10 inch pie pan with wrap on top side. Remove plastic wrap and trim edges to pan.

Fill prepared crust with apple filling (below). Roll other half into 12" circle utilizing same technique. Moisten edges of

*NOTE: 1 pound of apples yields about 3 cups chopped or 2 3/4 cups sliced apples.

lower crust with cold water, then transfer upper crust, pressing edges together, then form fluted edge. To prevent excessive browning, cover edges with foil tent or cover with a 2" or 3" strip of foil. Bake pie at 450°F. for 15 minutes; reduce heat to 375°F., then bake 40-50 minutes, removing the foil the last 15-20 minutes to brown.

Yield: 10" pie
Oven: 450°F./ 375°F.
Time: 40-50 minutes

CHERRY TOFU COBBLER

3 cups pitted fresh *or* frozen cherries
1 cup frozen unsweetened apple juice concentrate, thawed
1/2 cup unbleached flour
1/2 cup whole wheat flour
1 tsp. baking powder
4-5 ounces tofu
1 Tbsp. canola oil
1/2 cup nonfat dry milk, reconstituted
1/2 tsp. almond extract

Place pitted cherries with 3/4 cup of apple juice concentrate in medium saucepan and bring to a boil. Simmer for 5 minutes.

Place flour and baking powder in a food processor, then blend together. Add tofu, oil, milk, remainder of apple juice concentrate and almond extract to flour mixture, blending until smooth. Spray 9" x 9" pan with vegetable spray or other vegetable spray. Spread batter evenly in pan, then carefully cover with pitted cherries, pouring the juice over the top of the cherries. Bake for 45 to 50 minutes at 375°F.

Yield: 9 servings
Oven: 375°F.
Time: 40-45 minutes

STRAWBERRY PIE

8" baked pastry pie shell *or* 1 graham cracker crust
2 1/2 cups ripe fresh strawberries or frozen without sugar
1 Tbsp. unflavored gelatin
3/4 cup apple juice or pear apple juice
1 tsp. lemon juice
2 egg whites
1 cup whipped cream

Crush strawberries and add 1/4 cup apple juice. Soften gelatin in remaining 1/2 cup of apple juice and dissolve over low heat. Allow gelatin/juice mixture to cool slightly, then mix with berries and lemon juice. Chill, stirring occasionally until partially set. Beat egg whiles to form soft peaks. While gelatin mixture is still pourable, fold in egg whites, then whipped cream. Chill until strawberry filling forms mounds but not firmly. Pile high into a cool pie shell. Chill until firm. Trim with fresh berry halves.

Yield: 8" pie
Refrigerate

SUGARLESS PUMPKIN PIE FILLING

5 1/2 - 6 cups mashed cooked pumpkin (canned)
1 tsp. salt
3 1/2 cups skimmed evaporated milk
4 large eggs
1 Tbsp. unflavored gelatin
65 Equal tablets
5 Tbsp. honey
3 Tbsp. cinnamon
2 tsp. ginger
3 tsp. nutmeg
1 tsp. cloves
Whipped topping as desired

Dissolve Equal tablets in 1/4 cup of evaporated milk and gelatin in another 1/4 cup of evaporated milk. Heat oven to 425°F. Beat together eggs, salt, honey, cinnamon, ginger, nutmeg, cloves and pumpkin with rotary mixer, mixing well. Add the dissolved Equal tablets and gelatin (gelatin may be slightly lumpy) to other ingredients, mixing we. Slowly add milk, beating continuously to insure thorough mixing.

Pour into two prepared pastry lined pie pans. Bake for 45-55 minutes or just until a knife inserted into the filling comes out clean. The center may look soft, but will set later. Serve slightly warm or cold with whipped topping.

Yield: 2 - 10" pie fillings
Oven: 425⁰F.
Time: 45-55 minutes

CRAN-APPLE PIE

7 cups apples, peeled and sliced
1 cup cranberries
1 1/2 cups all fruit strawberry jam
1 1/2 tsp. cinnamon
1/4 tsp. ginger

TOPPING:

1 cup coconut or brown rice crispes
1/4 cup old fashioned oatmeal
2 Tbsp. honey
3/4 cup almonds, sliced

Combine apples, cranberries, jam and cinnamon. Place in pie plate.

Blend topping ingredients with steel blade in food processor. Crumble evenly over fruit pie. Bake until fruit is bubbly and the top is lightly browned.

Yield: 10 servings
Oven: 350⁰F.
Time: 45 minutes

SWEET POTATO PIE

9" pie crust
3 1/2 cups sweet potatoes, boiled soft (about 3 pounds)
1 cup skimmed evaporated milk *or* soymilk
3 eggs, beaten
1/2 cup maple syrup
2 1/2 tsp. cinnamon
1/4 tsp. cloves
1/2 tsp. allspice
1/4 tsp. nutmeg
1/4 tsp. ginger
1/4 tsp. salt

Wash potatoes and cook until soft with skins on. Using food processor with steel blade, blend sweet potatoes with other ingredients until batter is smooth. Pour into unbaked crust and bake at 450^0 F. for 10 minutes, then reduce temperature to 350^0 F. and bake for 45 minutes more or until knife comes out clean when inserted in center.

Yield: 9" pie
Oven: 450^0F. / 350^0F.
Time: 55 minutes

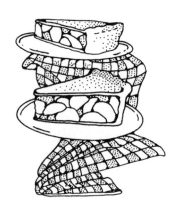

THIS N' THAT

THIS N' THAT

THIS N' THAT

HOMEMADE APPLESAUCE

8-12 apples to yield about 4 cups cooked
8-10 packages of Equal *
2 Tbsp. cinnamon
1/2 tsp. lemon juice
Dash nutmeg

Place uncooked apples in large pan, add about an inch of water, cover and cook until soft. Mash apples using a "molly" into large bowl, then dispose of peel, seeds, etc. Add Equal, cinnamon, nutmeg and lemon juice. Serve or package into bags and freeze.

Yield: 4 cups

* In place of Equal, substitute a 12 ounce can of unsweetened apple juice concentrate for water in large pan; if needed add more water to make the inch of water.

EASY HOMEMADE YOGURT (Keeps about 2 weeks)

1 quart water
1 tsp. vanilla
3 1/2 cups non-instant powdered milk
5 heaping Tbsp. plain yogurt
20 packages Equal or 36 tablets Equal
Starter---good, plain "live" Lactobacillus Acidophilus, Lactobacillus Bulgaricus, S. Thermophilus and B. Bifidum cultures

Combine water and milk, then heat to scalding. Allow to cool until comfortably warm or when you can slowly count to ten with your little finger in milk. While milk is cooling, take about 1/4 cup of warm milk and dissolve Equal in it. When milk is cool, add starter yogurt, vanilla and Equal; mix thoroughly. Pour into 5 cups with lids. Place in a pan large enough to hold all yogurt cups, then wrap pan and yogurt in heavy terry cloth towel. Process yogurt mixture in electric oven with light on until yogurt thickens like pudding about 8-10 hours. Do not peek at yogurt as it will not thicken; wait 8-9 hours, then look. After yogurt thickens, remove from oven. Allow to cool, then refrigerate. Often I make mine after dinner in evening, and it's ready when I get up.

Yield: 5 cups

HAM 'N SWISS QUICHE

1 cup grated Swiss cheese
1 cup finely chopped ham (Use food processor)
2 tsp. dried mint, crumbled
3 eggs, beaten
Dash pepper
12 oz. can evaporated skimmed milk
9 or 10 inch pie crust (Use Cheese-Rice Crust or a pastry crust)

Prepare ham and cheese. Add to pie crust. Roll mint in palm of hand to crumble into tiny bits and pieces. Sprinkle over cheese and ham. Beat eggs with a whip until frothy. Add milk to eggs, beating well; then pour over ham, cheese and mint. Bake until golden brown.

Yield: 4-6 servings
Oven: 400°F.
Time: 35-45 minutes

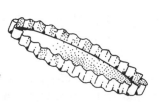

CHEESE-RICE PIE SHELL

1 1/2 cups cooked rice
1 egg, beaten
1/4 cup shredded cheese

Spray pie plate with vegetable cooking spray. Combine rice, egg and cheese, then press into pie plate. Bake 350°F. for 5 minutes. Press rice mixture up the sides with spoon, if necessary. Fill as desired--great for quiche.

Yield: 10" crust

SALADS AND POTATOES

CARROT PINEAPPLE SALAD

1 pound carrots, finely grated
20 oz. can crushed pineapple in its own juice
1 cup raisins (optional)
8 oz. container lemon yogurt

Mix all ingredients together. Chill for short time before serving.

Yield: About 4-5 cups

KB's GELLO

1 Box Sugar-Free Orange or Lime Jello
1 Box Sugar-Free Pineapple Jello
1 1/2 cups water
3/4 cup small curd cottage cheese
8 oz. carton plain or vanilla yogurt
8 oz. can crushed pineapple
1/2 cup chopped pecans
1/2 cup ice cold water

Bring 1 1/2 cups water to boil, then dissolve jello. Then add ice cold water, pineapple and cottage cheese. Add yogurt and pecans. Mix and pour into mold or individual cups.

Yield: 5-6 cups

SPICY APPLE-SWEET POTATOES

4 medium sweet potatoes, peeled and cut into 1/4 inch slices
    (about 5 cups)
3 cups cooking apples, peeled, cored and cut into wedges
1/2 cup apple juice
1 tsp. cornstarch *or* 1 tsp. arrowroot
1 1/2 tsp. ground cinnamon

Combine sweet potatoes, apples and 1/4 cup of apple juice in a 2 quart casserole dish. Microwave cook, uncovered, on high for 14-16 minutes, stirring occasionally or until potatoes and apples are crisp-tender.

In a small jar, combine remaining apple juice, cornstarch and cinnamon; replace jar lid and shake to combine ingredients. Stir into potato-apple mixture. Microwave, covered, on high for 2-3 minutes or until vegetables are glazed and heated through, stirring at least twice and rotating dish.

Yield: 8 Servings

TOPPINGS

APPLE TOPPING

3 cooking apples, peeled, cored and thinly sliced
1/2 cup apple juice concentrate
1/2 tsp. lemon juice
1/8 tsp. nutmeg
1/2 tsp. cinnamon
1 tsp. arrowroot

Dissolve arrowroot in apple juice concentrate. Then combine with remaining ingredients; bring to a boil. Cook over low heat 15-20 minutes, stirring frequently until apples are soft. Use for topping of waffles or as desired.

Yield: About 2 cups

BLUEBERRY SAUCE

1 1/2 cups blueberries, fresh **or** frozen
1/2 cup pineapple **or** apple juice concentrate
1 Tbsp. cornstarch

Combine berries and 1/4 cup juice concentrate in saucepan. Bring to a boil. Meanwhile, stir remaining juice into cornstarch **or** place juice in 8 ounce jar, keeping lid of jar within easy access, and add cornstarch, shake to mix. Over medium heat, add cornstarch mixture to berries, stirring until slightly thickened. *See note next page.*

Yield: 1 cup

NOTE:
1) For sweeter sauce add 3 Tbsp honey to berries with juice when combining in saucepan *or*
2) Use the Equal sweetener after sauce has been removed from heat and allowed to cool slightly. Add 2-4 packages of Equal, sweetening to taste.

PEACH PUREES

1 cup fresh or frozen peaches, peeled, pitted, and blended with 3 ounces apple juice concentrate
Raspberry Puree (see below)

On a 6 inch plate, spread one 2 ounce ladle full of peach puree evenly. Put 1 teaspoon raspberry puree in upper left hand corner of plate, in half-moon shape. Use a toothpick, and drag from inner part of raspberry puree towards outside of plate to make into a sun shape.

RASPBERRY PUREES: Use 1/2 cup raspberries pureed until smooth.

IMITATION "CREAM CHEESE" SPREAD

1 cup plain low fat yogurt
2 Tbsp. frozen unsweetened apple juice concentrate, thawed

With several layers of cheesecloth, line a strainer and place it over a small bowl. Place yogurt in cheesecloth and allow it to drain overnight in refrigerator (at least 8 hours, covering with plastic wrap in refrigerator. Remove the "cheese" from cloth and stir in apple juice. Then return to refrigerator, allowing it to rest several hours for flavors to blend. Use as a spread for toast or crackers or use in Layered Parfait Dessert.

Yield: 1 cup

STRAWBERRY JAM SPREAD

1 Tbsp. unflavored gelatin
1/2 cup unsweetened apple *or* white grape juice concentrate
4 cups fresh strawberries, washed, hulled and mashed *or*

frozen unsweetened strawberries, thawed + juice
1 1/2 tsp. lemon juice

Soften gelatin in 1/4 cup apple or grape juice concentrate, setting aside. Combine remaining apple or grape juice, strawberries, and lemon juice in saucepan. Bring to a boil, then reduce heat and simmer until soft (about 10-15 minutes), stirring very often. Add softened gelatin, stirring until completely dissolved. Remove from heat and allow to cool. Store in refrigerator.

Yield: 2 cups

CRAN-APPLE SAUCE

2 cups cranberries
1/2 cup frozen apple juice concentrate
3 cups unsweetened apple juice
2 Tbsp. orange juice concentrate
1/4 cup cornstarch

Wash berries, removing any that are brown. Combine 1 cup apple juice with cornstarch in 2 cup jar, replace lid and shake to mix/dissolve cornstarch. Then combine apple juice concentrate, orange juice with cornstarch apple juice mixture in medium saucepan. Stir in cranberries and cook until cranberries pop. Pour into serving dish, serving warm or cold.

Yield: About 2-2 1/2 cups

UNSWEETENED GRANOLA

4 cups rolled oats
1/2 cup wheat germ
1/2 cup unroasted sunflower *or* sesame seeds
1/3 cup unsweetened apple *or* white grape juice concentrate
1 tsp. vanilla
1/3 cup chopped dates
1/2 cup raisins
1/2 cup dried apples, chopped

Mix oats, wheat germ, and nuts. Combine juice concentrate and vanilla, then add to oat-wheat germ mixture. Place in 8" X 8" pan. Bake. Then add the dried apples, dates, and raisins to baked mix after taking out of oven. Use as desired with yogurt or cereal.

Yield: 6 cups
Oven: 275°F.
Time: 1 hour

LIGHT OAT WAFFLES

2 cups quick cooking rolled oats
1/4 cup oat bran
1 tsp. cinnamon
12 ounce can apple juice concentrate
3/4 cup water
3/4 tsp. ascorbic acid (Vitamin C) crystals
2 eggs, separated
1/2 tsp. salt
2 Tbsp. safflower oil
1/2 cup chopped walnuts or pecans, optional

Dissolve ascorbic acid in water; set aside. Mix oats, oat bran, apple juice concentrate, cinnamon, salt, egg yolk, and oil in blender until light and foamy; then add water mixture. Allow to sit for at least 10 minutes. Heat waffle iron. Put egg whites in a small bowl; beat the egg whites to <u>soft</u> peaks. After waffle iron is hot, beat batter vigorously. Stir in nuts and fold egg whites into batter gently, but thoroughly. Pour about a cup at a time onto hot waffle iron and spread to edges. Bake 10-15 minutes; be patient and don't peek the first 10 minutes. Serve hot with hot apples.

Yield: 5-6 waffles
Cook: 10-15 minutes

DRINKS

VANILLA SHAKE

1 cup non-fat milk liquid
3 pkg. Equal *or* 2-3 capsules glycine *or* 1 tsp. honey
4 ice cubes
1 tsp. vanilla
4 Tbsp. non-fat dry milk powder

Place all ingredients in blender except ice cubes. Blend slowly 30 seconds, then with blender on high speed, add ice cubes one at a time. Blend for 1 minute more. Serve.

Yield: 1 serving
Serve immediately

THICK CAROB SHAKE

1/2 cup low fat cottage cheese
3 pkg. Equal or 1 tsp. glycine powder
1/3 cup cold non-fat dry milk liquid
1 Tbsp. carob powder

Blend cottage cheese and carob powder in blender. Add Equal and milk. Blend until smooth. Pour in tall glass. Garnish with mint if desired.

Yield: 1 serving
Serve

Vanilla: Blend 1 tsp. vanilla with cottage cheese. Sprinkle lightly with nutmeg if desired.
Strawberry: Wash and remove stems. Put in blender with cottage cheese; blend until the strawberries are pureed. Garnish with a strawberry or with mint.

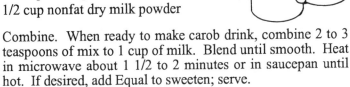

INSTANT HOT CAROB MIX

1/4 cup carob powder
1/2 cup nonfat dry milk powder

Combine. When ready to make carob drink, combine 2 to 3 teaspoons of mix to 1 cup of milk. Blend until smooth. Heat in microwave about 1 1/2 to 2 minutes or in saucepan until hot. If desired, add Equal to sweeten; serve.

Yield: 4-6 servings

CANDY / SNACKS

FUDGE

1/2 cup butter or safflower margarine
1/2 cup non-instant powdered dry milk
1/2 cup oat or rice flour
1 cup carob powder
2/3 cup plain or vanilla yogurt
1 Tbsp. honey
2 1/2 tsp. vanilla

Combine ingredients together. Beat with electric mixer. Place in 9" X 9" buttered pan. Refrigerate.

Yield: 9" X 9" pan

PEANUT CANDY

1 cup natural peanut butter (from health food store)
1/4 cup carob powder
1 small ripe banana, mashed
2 tsp. vanilla
Cinnamon
1/4 cup unsalted peanuts, finely minced

Mix ingredients together. Shape into 1" balls, and roll in cinnamon. Roll in finely minced peanuts. Store in airtight container and refrigerate.

Yield: dozen
Refrigerate

FIG FUDGE LOG

1/4 cup toasted sunflower seeds + 2/3 cup for roll
1 cup dates, chopped
8-10 dried figs, chopped
1/4 tsp. ascorbic acid crystals

In a food processor process 1/4 cup sunflowers briefly. Add dates, figs and ascorbic acid, processing until well chopped and mixture forms a ball. Form into a log shape, then roll in sunflower seeds. Cut as desired.

Yield: 9-12 servings

HOMEMADE TRAIL MIX

1 cup peanuts
2/3 cup apricots, diced
2/3 cup raisins
2/3 cup sunflower seeds
1/2 cup almonds
1/2 cup pecans
1/2 cup pumpkin seeds
1/2 cup cashews

Combine in large bowl. Store in large jar in refrigerator.

Yield: 5 cups

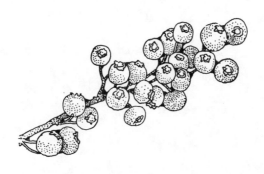

NO BAKE GRANOLA

2 cups oats, quick cooking
3/4 cup sunflower seeds
3/4 cup walnuts, chopped
3/4 cup dried apples
3/4 cup raisins

Combine in large bowl, half of the oats, walnuts, apples and raisins. Grind finely the remaining half of the oats and sunflower seeds in a food processor. Then add to large bowl, tossing to combine. Store in glass jar in refrigerator.

Yield: 7-8 servings

OTHER

BAKING POWDER *

1/3 cup potassium bicarbonate
2/3 cup cream of tartar
2/3 cup arrowroot

Mix, sift and store in jar.

Yield: 2 cups

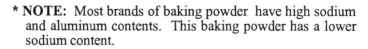

* **NOTE:** Most brands of baking powder have high sodium and aluminum contents. This baking powder has a lower sodium content.

SIMPLE WAYS TO REDUCE INTAKE
OF FATS AND CALORIES

You can often reduce the calories, fat and the amount of cholesterol in your cooking without compromising the results by simply making substitutions or leaving unnecessary ingredients out when following a recipe. If you are unsure of an ingredient, try cutting the amount in half. Experimentation is the name of the game.

TRY USING:

- **RAISINS, DRIED, FRUIT, AND BANANAS** to add sweetness to recipes and reduce fat or oil.
- **YOGURT** for SOUR CREAM
- **SKIMMED OR NON-FAT DRY MILK** for WHOLE MILK
- **SKIMMED EVAPORATED MILK** in place of the usual EVAPORATED MILK
- **HONEY** in place of SUGAR by using a 1:2 ratio of honey to sugar, then slightly reducing (usually by 1/4th) the liquid portion of the recipe.
- **CAROB POWDER** in place of COCOA
- **CAROB CHIPS** for CHOCOLATE CHIPS
- **WHOLE WHEAT FLOUR** for WHITE FLOUR. Either substitute the same amount, or for a lighter effect, mix WHOLE WHEAT FLOUR AND UNBLEACHED FLOUR in equal amounts.
- **CANOLA OIL** for OIL. Canola oil is a monosaturated fat, the same as olive oil. It is considered a "good" oil.
- **ARROWROOT OR TAPIOCA** for CORNSTARCH.
- **FRESH FRUIT** instead of CANNED FRUIT. If you do use canned fruit, buy FRUIT CANNED IN ITS OWN JUICE or in another fruit juice or water.
- **MORE FIBER** to delay absorption and to counteract the effects of sugar. Increased fiber also brings a significant amount of micro-nutrients, particularly chromium, into the diet.
- **EGG WHITES** for WHOLE EGGS.
- **FORTIFIED FLAX** for EGGS.
- **APPLESAUCE , BANANAS, or NON-FAT BUTTERMILK** for part or all OIL in recipes to reduce fat.

EQUIVALENTS OR SUBSTITUTIONS

1/2 cup carob powder = 1/3 cup cocoa

3 Tbsp. carob powder +
2 Tbsp water +   = 1 oz. chocolate
2 tsp. oil

1 tsp. arrowroot = 1 tsp. cornstarch

1 cup white rice = 1 cup brown rice

1 cup uncooked rice = 3 cups cooked rice

1 cup butter = 2/3 cup oil

2 Tbsp. agar flakes = 1 Tbsp. gelatin

12 oz. can frozen juice = 1 1/2 cup thawed juice

1/4 tsp. baking soda +
1/2 tsp. cream of tartar = 1 tsp. baking powder

1 pound flour = 4 cups flour

1 pound raisins = 2 3/8 cups raisins

1 pound dates = 1 3/4 cups chopped dates

1 pound apples = 3 cups sliced apples

1 whole lemon rind = 1 Tbsp. grated rind

1 pound figs = 2 1/2 cups chopped figs

1 medium lemon = 3 Tbsp. lemon juice

1 lb.unshelled walnuts = 1 1/2 -1 3/4 cups shelled walnuts

1/4 lb. nuts = 1 cup chopped nuts

1 lb. rice = 2 1/3 cups rice

1 cup nonfat milk
+ 1 Tbsp. vinegar   = 1 cup buttermilk

ALLERGY SUBSTITUTIONS

1 cup soymilk +
1 Tbsp. vinegar or lemon juice   = 1 cup buttermilk
   (Allow to stand 5 minutes before using)

2/3 cup brown rice syrup   = 1/2 cup honey
   (Reduces sweetness in recipes. About half as sweet as sugar).

Apple juice   = milk in most recipes.

1/4 tsp. Vitamin C crystals   = 1 Tbsp. lemon juice
   (sago palm)

1 cup date sugar   = 1 cup sugar
   (Good for breads, muffins, cakes-mix with liquid and allow to stand a few minutes)

1/2 cup honey   = 1 cup sugar - 1/4th liquid

1 cup Fruit Source liquid   = 1 cup honey
   (white grape juice + brown rice)

1 cup Fruit Source granules   = 1 cup sugar

1 to 1 1/2 egg whites   = 1 large egg

1 1/2 tsp. Ener-G Egg Replacer +   = 1 egg
2 Tbsp. water

1 cup applesauce or mashed banana   = 1 cup butter *or* margarine
   (best in breads, cakes, muffins, biscuits)

1 tsp. fortified flax + 3 tsp. water   = 1 egg
   (mix together and allow to soak for 30 minutes)

3/4 cup fruit juice or milk   = 1 cup oil
   (Reduce oven by 25°F.)

3/4 cup pumpkin or butternut squash = 1 cup butter, margarine
   (Reduce oven by 25°F.)

FLOURS

For 1 cup flour use:

Stone ground whole wheat 1/2 cup + unbleached stone ground flour 1/2 cup

Spelt flour, cup for cup

Kamut flour, cup for cup

Amaranth (good for baking) 1/4 cup + 3/4 cup rice *or* oat flour
or 3/4 cup amaranth flour + 1/4 cup tapioca starch *or* potato flour

Brown rice flour (good for cookies & pie crusts) 1/2 cup + 1/2 cup oat flour

INDEX

Call 1-800-669-CALM
--------------To Order --------------

Please Print

Name_____

Addres_____

City_____State_____Zip _____

BOOKS

The Anxiety Epidemic (Dr. Billie J. Sahley)	$9.95
Breaking Your Addiction Habit book (Drs. B. Sahley & K. Birkner)	$8.95
Malic Acid and Magnesium for Fibromyalgia and Chronic Pain	$3.95
(Dr. Billie J. Sahley)	
Natural Way To Control Hyperactivity book *(Dr. Billie J. Sahley)*	$7.95
Chronic Emotional Fatigue (Dr. Billie J. Sahley)	$3.95
The Melatonin Report (Dr. Billie J. Sahley)	$3.95
Healing With Amimo Acids ((Drs. B. Sahley & K. Birkner)	$5.95
Breaking The Sugar Habit Cookbook (Dr. K. Birkner)	$5.95

AUDIO CASSETTES by Dr. Billie J. Sahley - $10 Each

Anxiety	Fear
Anxiety/ Panic Attacks - Causes & Control	Forgiving and Healing
	Guilt
Anger	Letting Go
Being, Your Way	Hyperactivity - Causes & Control
Communication	Phobias
Depression	Therapeutic Uses of Amino Acids
Escape	(Drs. Sahley & Birkner)

Catalog (No Shipping Charge / Free with Purchase) $3 _____

SUBTOTAL _____

Texas Residents ADD 7.75% Sales Tax _____

Shipping (first item $3 + $1 subsequent)** _____

TOTAL**_____

Personal Checks are held for 10 working days. To expedite order, send money order.

MC / Visa / Discover _ _ _ _ - _ _ _ _ - _ _ _ _ - _ _ _ _

Signature_____

Send To: **Pain & Stress Therapy Center**
5282 Medical Drive #160 San Antonio, TX 78229-6023

** Canadian & Other Foreign Countries ADD $8 to the above amounts.
We accept World Money Orders or MC / Visa Discover ONLY!

About the Author

Kathy Birkner is a Pain Therapist at the Pain & Stress Center in San Antonio. She is a Registered Nurse, Certified Registered Nurse Anesthetist, Registered Massage Therapist, and Orthomolecular Therapist. She is a Diplomate in the American Academy of Pain Management. She attended Brackenridge Hospital School of Nursing, University of Texas at Austin, Southwest Missouri State University, and Clayton University. She holds degrees in nursing, nutrition, and behavior therapy. Dr. Birkner has done graduate studies through the Center for Integral Medicine and U.C.L.A. Medical School under the direction of Dr. David Bresler. Additionally, she has studied advanced nutritional biochemistry through Jeffrey Bland, Ph.D, Director of HealthComm. She is a member of American Association of Nurse Anesthetists, Texas Association of Nurse Anesthetists, American Association of Pain Management, American College of Osteopathic Pain Management and Sclerotherapy, and American Association of Counseling and Development. She is author of *Breaking Your Sugar Habit Cookbook* and co-author with Dr. Sahley of *Breaking Your Addiction Habit* and *Healing With Amino Acids* books and *Therapeutic Uses of Amino Acids* audio cassette tape.